Culture, Architecture and Nature

Gathering his most compelling essays and addresses from the last fifty years in one accessible volume, this book looks at the pioneering ideas that underpin Sim Van der Ryn's ecological design philosophy. It offers a unique decade-by-decade retrospective of the key issues in environmental design, beginning with the most recent years and looking back to the sixties. With an introductory chapter and further reading for each decade, this book is key reading for any architect or designer practicing today, and students will find a wealth of knowledge with which to support their studies. The author's beautiful illustrations, painted in a corresponding timescale to the chapters, offer further insight into the way he understands the challenges of humanity's stewardship of our planet.

Sim Van der Ryn is the president of EcoDesign Collaborative, a Northern California firm known for its pioneering work in integral design. For over 30 years he taught architecture and design at the University of California, Berkeley, inspiring a new generation to create buildings and communities that are sensitive to place, climate, and the flow of human interactions. As California State Architect in the seventies he was responsible for designing and building the first series of energy efficient, people-friendly, climate responsive government buildings. He is the author of six groundbreaking books about planning and design, which have helped inspire architects to see the myriad ways they can apply physical and social ecology to architecture and environmental design. Van der Ryn lives in the San Francisco Bay area.

"Glimpse into the genealogy of one of the pioneers of the 'sustainability ethic' that has now captured the hearts and minds of built environment practitioners. Maybe you never had the chance to cross paths with Sim Van der Ryn; you were busy, far away, or born in a different time and place that didn't allow for this particular serendipity to grace you. Wander through Sim's speeches. Appreciate the consistent, gentle, tenacious message that runs throughout early Sim to recent Sim. Our goal as designers is to evolve; observing Sim's evolution provides a model of hope, perseverance, and dignity. Lean on this book for inspiration, comfort, and courage."

Jane Talkington, Sustainability Scholar-in-Residence, Institute of Creativity and Innovation, Spears School of Business, Oklahoma State University

Culture, Architecture and Nature

An Ecological Design Retrospective

Sim Van der Ryn

Edited by Richard Olsen

First published 2014
by Routledge
2 Park Square, Milton Park, Abingdon, Oxon, OX14 4RN

Simultaneously published in the USA and Canada
by Routledge
711 Third Avenue, New York, NY 10017

Routledge is an imprint of the Taylor & Francis Group, an informa business

© 2014 Sim Van der Ryn

The right of Sim Van der Ryn to be identified as author of this work has been asserted by him in accordance with sections 77 and 78 of the Copyright, Designs and Patents Act 1988.

All rights reserved. No part of this book may be reprinted or reproduced or utilized in any form or by any electronic, mechanical, or other means, now known or hereafter invented, including photocopying and recording, or in any information storage or retrieval system, without permission in writing from the publishers.

Trademark notice: Product or corporate names may be trademarks or registered trademarks, and are used only for identification and explanation without intent to infringe.

British Library Cataloguing in Publication Data
A catalogue record for this book is available from the British Library

Library of Congress Cataloging-in-Publication Data
Van der Ryn, Sim.
[Essays. Selections]
Culture, architecture and nature : an ecological design retrospective / Sim=
 Van der Ryn.
pages cm
Includes bibliographical references and index.
1. Architecture--Environmental aspects. I. Title.
NA737.V36A35 2013
720'.47--dc23
2013013461

ISBN13: 978-0-415-83966-2 (hbk)
ISBN13: 978-0-415-83967-9 (pbk)
ISBN13: 978-1-31588-545-2 (ebk)

All illustrations © Sim Van der Ryn, photographic reproductions by Dusan Mills – Alien Lifeform Research

Typeset in Adobe Caslon Pro 10/12 pt by Fakenham Prepress Solutions, Fakenham, Norfolk NR21 8NN

I like to build places
Where nature is the foreground
That cannot be overpowered
By our temporary creations.

I use geometry not only
To organize space and to mark
The social interactions within
But also to resonate with
The landscape.

The building is not a fixed
Object but part of the larger
Pattern that flows with change
A permeable living membrane
Responding to change.

I like to use natural materials
Native to a place
As well as advanced technology
And scientific intelligence.

Architecture is part of the process
Of "re-membering"—putting back
Together our collective dreams.
I like to design buildings that are
Places for learning, healing, reflection.

The building should tell a story
About people and place
And be a pathway to understanding
Ourselves within nature.

Contents

Acknowledgments ix
Books by Sim Van der Ryn x
Introduction: Nature's Mad as Hell xi

PART 1
The Two-Thousands and Beyond: A New Radicalism Towards the Integral Paradigm   **3**

"Transformation," Keynote, Cascadia Green Building Council, Seattle, WA, 2009   7

Athena Award Reception Speech, Congress for the New Urbanism, San Francisco, CA, 2008   11

Keynote, Environmental Design Research Association, Sacramento, CA, 2007   18

"Greening Campuses, Greening Education," Los Angeles, CA, 2006   22

Further Reading: The Seminal Books of the Two-Thousands and Beyond   28

PART 2
The Nineties: Integrating the Ecologies of Nature, Culture, and Humans   **31**

Keynote, Solar Energy Association of Oregon, Twentieth Anniversary Conference, Portland, OR, 1999   36

"Healthy Building," *Resurgence*, March–April 1993   40

CONTENTS

Keynote, First Los Angeles Ecological Cities Conference, University of California, Los Angeles, 1991   47

Presentation in Dialogue with Christopher Alexander, Esalen Institute, Big Sur, CA, 1991   61

Further Reading: The Seminal Books of the Nineties   63

PART 3
The Eighties: The Lost Decade   65

"Integral Design," Sausalito, CA, 1988   69

"The Next Urban Transformation," Sausalito, CA, 1985   85

"Little America," *Le Monde*, 1981   89

Further Reading: The Seminal Books of the Eighties   99

PART 4
The Seventies: The Environmental Awakening and Response   101

Bateson Building Dedication, Sacramento, CA, 1979   105

"Ecotopia Now: Utopia Brought Down to Earth," *New Age*, 1979   108

"The Coming Age of Natural Design," *L'Architecture d'Aujourd'hui*, March 1975   126

Further Reading: The Seminal Books of the Seventies   133

PART 5
The Sixties: Questioning the Dominant World View, Ethos, and Paradigm   135

"Building a People's Park," Berkeley, CA, 1969   139

"Problems and Puzzles," *AIA Journal*, January 1966   148

Further Reading: The Seminal Books of the Sixties   154

Index   155

Acknowledgments

Over a long career, I have written hundreds of published pieces on architecture and design. The birth of this book was initiated by my beloved partner, Francine Allen, a gifted author, editor, and writing teacher who, in leafing through my archives, suggested that we collect the best, most relevant pieces and publish them as a collection. I invited Richard Olsen, a talented, experienced architectural editor and author, to design, develop, and format the collection. Through fortunate coincidence, Dusan Mills, a former client and friend, offered to photograph my watercolours, produced over the years, which I had never exhibited. We included them in the proposal, to provide a visual glimpse of how I view the world.

My special thanks to the team at Taylor & Francis and Production Editor Alanna Donaldson for their patience, competence, and open-heartedness in bringing this work into the world. A month long residency granted by the Rockefeller Foundation to us at their Center in Bellagio on Lake Como, Italy, provided a beautiful, inspiring, and calm setting to complete the book's final edit and production phase. My thanks to the Bellagio Director, Pilar Palacia, and to Rob Garris, the Foundation's New York Program Director.

Books by Sim Van der Ryn

Design for Life: The Architecture of Sim Van der Ryn, Gibbs Smith Publisher, 2005

Ecological Design (with Stuart Cowan), Island Press, 1996

Sustainable Communities: A New Design Synthesis for Cities, Suburbs and Towns (with Peter Calthorpe), Sierra Club Books, 1986

The Integral Urban House: Self-Reliant Living in the City (with Bill and Helga Olkowski), Sierra Club Books, 1977

The Toilet Papers, Chelsea Green Publishing, 1977

Farallones Scrapbook, Random House, 1971

Dorms at Berkeley: An Environmental Analysis (with Murray Silverstein), Center for Planning and Development Research, University of California, 1967

Introduction: Nature's Mad As Hell!

> My life in design has, from the beginning, been driven by questioning the implicit assumptions that propel design ... I'm often called a pioneer: "a person who first enters or settles a region." That region exists in the heart and the mind. I rejected formal religion as a child, and later the worship of Progress and an unquestioning faith in materialist mechanistic science and technology ... I have faith in the possibility of human culture and consciousness transcending a long obsession with objects, quantities, and control, moving toward an ecological intelligence and compassion for everything that is alive and changing, including each of us. The heart of ecological design is not efficiency or sustainability. It is the embodiment of animating spirit, the soul of the living world as embodied in each of us waiting to be reborn and expressed in what we design ... We are waiting to be re-enchanted—to join our higher selves, our souls, to the evolving living world.
> —Sim Van der Ryn, from *Design for Life*, 2005

This retrospective work incorporates essays and talks focusing on environmental design and its relation to people, culture, nature, politics, education, and the institutions that shape our lives. Here, I connect the dots of my work as a designer, teacher, writer, and artist, sharing with you the evolution of my ideas, thought experiments, worldview, philosophy, and values, as presented in selected essays and talks from over the last 50 years.

The essential adventure of our time is what I call "The Great Turning," the shift from an industrial-growth society to a life-sustaining civilization. I've been on this design journey most of my life, bouncing along through hope, some accomplishments, and occasional despair, as the question of "Can we do it?" is always there. Forty years ago, E.F. Schumacher, author of *Small is Beautiful*, gave us a useful answer:

> Can we rely on it that a "turning around" will be accomplished by enough people quickly enough to save the modern world? This question is often asked, but whatever answer is given to it will mislead. The answer "yes" would lead to complacency; the answer "no" to despair. It's desirable to leave these perplexities behind us and get down to work.

I recently saw filmmaker Werner Herzog's documentary *Cave of Forgotten Dreams*, the story of the Chauvet Caves in Southern France. These dwellings, discovered in recent times, were home to humans 30,000 years ago. The beautiful charcoal animal drawings that cover their walls span a period of 20,000 years. Think about it. Seven hundred generations of humans used these ritual spaces. The Industrial Age is 200 years old, or only seven generations of humans, and in that time we have transformed the entire living Earth in drastic and dire ways that threaten our future.

We know the bad news: A weird, chaotic climate, which, even if we stopped spewing any carbon into the atmosphere tomorrow, will continue its erratic path for many generations; the continued destruction of critical global ecosystems—forests, oceans, fertile soils, and wetlands; and the loss of indigenous pre-industrial communities and cultures. Meanwhile, the toxic pollution of air, water, soil, and our bodies continues, in spite of the laws created in the 1970s as the result of Earth Day. In my lifetime, planetary population has grown from two billion to seven billion people. A consequence of population growth, a declining and degraded resource base, and excess consumption and waste in the richest countries is endless wars over access to resources. Global capitalism systematically steals nature's wealth and converts it to riches for the very few, while also destroying a global commons that belongs to everyone. Big money has bought our democracy and turned elections into auctions in which a small oligarchy of corporate billionaires compete to buy politicians.

Recent findings in cognitive science and neurology confirm that both emotion and reason originate in the frontal cortex of the brain. A recent study of people's attitudes towards climate change found no correlation between a subject's level of education in science and whether or not a subject believed that climate change and global warming are caused by human action. Emotion and ideology may determine what we choose to accept as truth rather than cold facts or widely accepted scientific evidence.

At a recent American Academy for the Advancement of Science conference, experts agreed that the path to a truly sustainable future is through the muddy waters of emotions, values, ethics, and imagination. As one speaker said, "We don't live in the real world, we live in the world we imagine … and if we can't imagine a better world, we won't get it. This imagining will be complex and difficult. Sustainability covers far more than scientific facts; it also incorporates how we relate to nature and ourselves." Societies' choices are driven by people's cultural perceptions of reality. Science is part of the problem. If the sustainability discussion is largely in scientific language, it will narrow people's vision of what's possible.

Our society appears to be in a condition I call "rigid instability." Our major institutions—government and politics, the economy, the media, education, and health care—are in trouble. Scale is part of the problem. Our institutions, whether on a national or global scale, are too large and cumbersome, each lacking accountability or transparency. Out of the financial crisis of 2008, we were told the banks were "too big to fail," and we paid to bail them out. Many of our institutions have become too big NOT to fail. The institutions we know as "nation states," particularly those covering large parts of several continents such as the U.S., China, and Russia, are particularly vulnerable to rigid instability. They are ruled by small oligarchies that hold most of the wealth. The largest nation states include diverse ethnic and cultural groups and diverse and vastly different ecosystems, and no single policy structure or ideology can fit all people or all ecosystems. The unique qualities of regionally shared physical and cultural commons are sacrificed to the false God called Progress. Perhaps the largest nations will devolve into interconnected regions, each with their own economies and governance. (Regions are identified by their unique geography, ecosystems, natural resources, and human and natural histories.) The global reach of technology and economics tends to ignore the values of regional difference, creating what James Kunstler has labeled "a geography of nowhere."

We live in descriptions of reality, not reality itself. Jared Diamond's book *Collapse*, Charles Mann's *1491*, and Amy Chua's *Day of Empire* are recent works that tell the story of great societies throughout history that collapsed because their rigid structures of belief could not adapt to new challenges. Through their rigid denial they overshot their ecological base.

Rigid structures, both mental and physical, are unstable because they don't adapt easily to change. We need to create Resilient Communities. "Resilient," my dictionary says, means "to spring back, rebound, the ability to return to original form after having been compressed or stretched … recovery from illness, depression, adversity."

The most fundamental problem that affects everything was the leap toward a modern world 300 years ago. It was fueled by the European view of early science and philosophy that our bodies and minds were separate entities, and that we humans were separate from and above nature. The twentieth century began with an event in the then-emerging world of modern science that few are aware of: the battle between the Physicalists and Vitalists in the German universities. The Physicalists maintained that only phenomena that could be physically scrutinized and measured were the legitimate object of scientific study, while the Vitalists maintained that beyond the strictly measurable physical world there were vital forces beyond physical/material description.

Physicalist materialist science won, and students had to take an oath in blood, swearing to uphold the physicalist ideology. This has led us to a modern world in which the destruction of the natural world is justified in the name of Progress for the human world.

Ironically, our world relies entirely on a living world of millions of species and their complex interactions. Forty years ago, one of my mentors, a psychiatrist and naturalist, called the Progress process, "Burning down the house of life in order to toast marshmallows." The great disconnect between nature and our culture's materialist paradigm is unraveling and burning up the living systems that support our lives.

The disconnect between what is truly alive and what is not creates increasingly strange outcomes such as the U.S. Supreme Court ruling that "corporations are people." People are alive and, thus, part of the living world of nature. Corporations are not alive.

In order to create a future for ourselves, we will need to take radical and bold steps. There are no easy answers to solving the many problems we face. With his book *Free Radicals*, British physicist and journalist Michael Brooks seeks to provide a counter narrative to popular interpretations of the scientific world that emphasize science's predictability, blandness, and affinity with constituted power. He does this by considering a number of examples in the history of science and by looking at the lives of particular scientists—scenarios that demonstrate how science's practice is often, at its heart, an "anarchic, creative, and radical endeavor." Science can be more than what we imagine to be the product of rational, logical positivist consciousness. Such a revelation is shocking, perhaps, to those for whom science is a field marked by routine and discipline.

The birth of the Modern architecture movement at the beginning of the twentieth century enthusiastically embraced a philosophy of ignoring the qualities of place in favor of bold new form statements based on the technologies of glass, steel, concrete, and the availability of cheap fossil fuels and electricity to heat and light this new "International Style." It reflected the hopeful optimism of a European generation of architects after World War I to replace the Imperial architecture of the old order with a more socially and regionally equalizing architecture based on advances in technology. Unfortunately, the best of intentions often have unintended consequences. In the post World War II world, Modernism spread everywhere, but the social and human values held by its founders were often sacrificed to the dogma of "Modern style," regardless of the qualities of place or function.

I started teaching in a university architecture program more than 50 years ago, having gotten interested in architecture as a teenager who worked summers on New England farms and, one particular summer, as a teen that helped a 19-year-old handyman (with two kids) build a Cape Cod cottage from a set of stock plans. The process of going from drawings to three-dimensional reality was fascinating. Later, while in architecture school, during another summer break I was fortunate to work on a project with Buckminster Fuller, one of his space frame systems, that was then being built in the school's courtyard. During the same period, I also worked on a mobile house that had many features designed around reducing water use and capturing solar heat—things totally novel in those days. So when I started teaching, my interest in design was not grounded in theoretical concepts and ideology but more in what I called "thought experiments," which to me meant testing ideas through built models, not just drawing them. (I was frustrated by what I called "the Howard Roark Syndrome," an approach to architecture based on Ayn Rand's book *The Fountainhead* that idolizes the lone creative genius who is determined to foist his great ideas on an unknowing public. In June 1963, in a paper I delivered at a national seminar on the Teaching of Architecture, held at Cranbrook Academy, I addressed this subject:

> We have put our faith in a curriculum which attempts to do just that which it cannot do: produce the creative or intuitive genius … We tend to judge creativity in architecture not in terms of how well a problem has been solved, but rather by a judgment of the apparent physical solution—the personal stylistic signature. We have stressed product rather than process … The design sequences of our schools have become little more than a 10-semester course in architectural cartooning.

That was said before Postmodernism, Deconstructivism, and all the other "ideo-isms" that have sprung up in the last 50 years in architecture, each of which has been mirrored in the design studios of the most prestigious architecture schools internationally. It continues today. Of course hand drawing has been replaced with computer programs, which, when handled with deft student fingers, yield an empty colorful stream of architectural fantasies. Patrik Schumacher, writing in the British *Architectural Review*, "sees no future for the type of hopelessly unrealistic education lauded by the British architectural establishment."

"The submissions to the current RIBA President's Medals," Schumacher says,

> demonstrate once more that architectural education in Britain is operating in a parallel universe. The (best?) students of the current generation as well as their teachers seem to think that the ordinary life processes of contemporary society are too boring to merit the avant-garde's attention. Instead we witness the invention of scenarios that are supposedly more interesting than the challenges actually posed by contemporary reality. The points of departure for the majority of projects are improbable narratives with intended symbolic message or poetic import … The result might be a provocation at best, but often ends up as nothing but naive (if not pompous) posturing. Success in the world is not to be expected from such pursuits.

The demonstration of creative imagination and virtuoso visualization skills is not enough to merit an award. Should we not expect the best students and teachers at the best architecture schools to make a serious contribution to the innovative upgrading of the discipline's capacity to take on the challenges it might actually face via its future clients and commissions?

There are architecture schools that do have programs that involve practical and innovative hands-on design and construction by students, such as the Annual Solar Decathlon competition. And there are organizations that provide design services to the vast majority of the world's population that are off the radar screen of our profession. What they do and how they work needs to be integrated into a design education that is so insulated from the reality of how most of the world lives.

DesignActivism.net surveys and lists sources that deal with design activism, which I take to mean books, programs, and projects that go beyond the prevailing "business as usual" in architecture and design. A 2010 posting on the Design Activism site lists about 60 sources, mostly books. One of them started as a project to connect designers interested in a design revolution and resulted in a groundbreaking book, *Design Revolution* by Emily Pilloton. It presents innovative product designs in eight areas: water, health, energy, education, mobility, food, play, and enterprise. Pilloton, an industrial designer and a UC Berkeley architecture graduate, went on the road in the U.S. to architecture and design schools and high schools to show examples of these products. With help from her partner, she also began a program in a rural North Carolina school district working with students to remodel classrooms and do a variety of community construction projects. We need projects like hers to go viral. Most design is for the 1 percent: the people, corporations, and government that can afford it. What we need most is design for the other 99 percent, or 90 percent of the people on the planet, who have no access to modern, intelligent, ecologically grounded design.

We need to downsize the scale of things to a manageable level where people can come together to creatively solve common problems and help each other. We need to redesign for the human scale of local community.

Perhaps this country, now only 250 years old, just grew too fast and we never took the time to know where we were. Growing up, I watched the interstate highway system being built and farmland and open space turned into ticky tack boxes, and they all looked the same, as the song goes. Real communities are place based and grow organically over time, not mechanical templates stamped out on a map. America's greatest liability is our continent-wide suburbanization.

The three "R"s for twenty-first century design are restoration, regeneration, and resiliency. This means integrating building design within a larger context of community design and the integral ecological design of food, water, energy, and recycling systems, at every scale. Today's middle school students know the mantra "materials cycle, energy flows, life webs." Today's designers need to imprint it into their awareness. The interactions between the natural world and built environments are far too complex to lend themselves to simple metrics such as the term "sustainability" suggests.

The compelling overall theme in this book is the long search for a unified approach to the design of systems—both built and natural—and integrating scales ranging from the molecular to the global. Science has confirmed the Gaia Hypothesis developed by atmospheric scientist James Lovelock and microbiologist Lynn Margulis that Earth is a single living, self-regulating organism composed of interconnected life forms that cooperate to maintain ecological balance. This is in contrast to the neo-Darwinian thesis—that life is based around competition and survival of the fittest. Nature's geometry is fractal at every scale, from our galaxy to the geometry of air and water movement, from global weather systems to the spiral whirl spinning down your shower drain.

The nutrients, energy, and information essential to life flow smoothly across scales ranging from bacteria to continents. If we are to include ecological concerns within design, we must discover ways to integrate our design processes across multiple levels of scale. Ecological design becomes the meta-discipline overriding the narrow mentality and obtuse language of dozens of separate scientific, technical, and design disciplines.

Frank Lloyd Wright once said, "The heart is the first feature of working minds." Just as we need to always be aware that nature's flows and cycles must be integral to what we design, we need always to be aware that we are nature. When we forget that body and mind are integral, and we isolate what we imagine to be our thinking mind in small areas of our brain, we deny our own humanity—our deepest intelligence, creativity, and understanding. We must remember that we are part of the very nature mechanarchy is destroying.

The brilliant systems analyst Donella Meadows wrote a famous paper in 1997 called "Twelve Leverage Points to Intervene in a System." She points out that most people think the highest point of leverage to change a system are numbers such as costs, profits, subsidies, taxes, and standards. Numbers are the most clearly perceived, but they rarely change behaviors and therefore have little long-term effect. Next come metrics such as material stocks and flows, the structure of information flow, the rules of the system.

The most critical place to change a system lies with challenging fundamental assumptions—the power to transcend our existing unchallenged paradigms, or what we believe to be true about how things are. The mindset, or dominant paradigm, is powerful when its unstated assumptions are shared. We are in a time when the "Growth/Progress/Materialistic/Individualist" paradigm is collapsing. So leave your normal thinking minds behind and do what the Greeks did. Do the "thoumos thump:" rhythmically pound your sternum just below the neck, behind which lies your thymus gland—a control center in the distribution of T cells that maintain your immune system. The Greeks considered this place the location of one's soul. So activate your soul and engage your full minds and hearts in our common shared journey to promote life and beauty.

Yes, it's true: You can't connect the dots of your life before you have lived them. I've had a successful and gratifying life as a teacher and designer, but I was often in two places: Wherever I was in space and time, and then somewhere else in my head. As a designer, I was always driven to find solutions. Design solutions are far easier to find than solutions to the problems we face in our lives. That takes time. Modern culture has thrived through the development of our left-brain capacity to reduce all problems to finite, rational solution algorithms. But the design problems we face consist of multi-dimensional, complex systems issues that cross traditional disciplines and knowledge sets. We need to develop whole new mindsets, ways of working together, communicating across mindsets, tossing away old habits and inventing new collaborative processes to overcome today's fragmented mentality. We need to shift our focus from "interdisciplinary" to "meta-disciplinary," an integrated whole systems approach. You can't think "out of the box," because thinking is the box.

The most used noun in our everyday conversations is "time." In a multitude of ways, we are obsessed and driven by it. Our lives today remind me of when you fast-forward a movie download to 4, 8, or 16 times its normal speed. We race around, drowning in information and imagery. Next, next,

next. Our eyes dart around, but are we truly seeing? With all our speedy need to get on with the next thing, we never catch up. Are we ever truly present? We're connected but how, and to whom, what, and why?

The simple pleasures of peace and quiet seem to be the rarest of commodities, and in our present environment indeed they are. A recent piece by Pico Iyer in the *New York Times* gives us a powerful picture of how our new information/communication technologies make finding that peace so much more difficult:

> In barely one generation we've moved from exulting in the time-saving devices that have so expanded our lives to trying to get away from them—often in order to make more time. The more ways we have to connect, the more many of us seem desperate to unplug. Like teenagers, we appear to have gone from knowing nothing about the world to knowing too much all but overnight … We have more and more ways to communicate, as Thoreau noted, but less and less to say. Partly because we're so busy communicating. And—as he might also have said—we're rushing to meet so many deadlines that we hardly register that what we need most are lifelines.

So what to do? The central paradox of the machines that have made our lives so much brighter, quicker, longer, and healthier is that they cannot teach us how to make the best use of them. A series of tests in recent years has shown that after spending time in quiet rural settings subjects "exhibit greater attentiveness, stronger memory and generally improved cognition. Their brains become both calmer and sharper." More than that, empathy, as well as deep thought, depends (as neuroscientists like Antonio Damasio have found) on neural processes that are "inherently slow." The very ones our high-speed lives have little time for.

We humans are no different than the 700 generations of humans who lived in those French caves 30,000 years ago. We were designed to thrive in a natural world. Our wiring is designed to respond quickly to immediate threats, not to longer-term change. It's interesting that what Robert Graves called "mechanarchy" swept the world in the early twentieth century, when art moved from a genteel realist tradition to a much more primitive expression, as in the work of Picasso, whose bulls seem to be channeling the Chauvet caves. So with all our material comforts and technology but with an overload of demands on our time and neural pathways, we're less adjusted, perhaps, to our overstressed lives than the cave men were to their existence. Maybe while the tentacles of the powerful, centrally organized scientific and mechanically structured world destroys the living world and its complexity beyond today's science, it is also destroying our very humanity?

For me, reconnecting to myself is congruent with reconnecting to the natural world. This day in February it is raining for the first time in many weeks. The rains here in coastal Northern California generally start after Thanksgiving and continue into spring. This year, little rain. Last December, it rained every day. This December, not one day, and it was sunny and warm consistently, in what is normally a rainy, cold month. With a fire going in the hearth, I'm happy to be writing at my computer, which I avoided when the sun was shining. But with the weird weather and the knowledge that, for the rest of many lifetimes, these conditions will probably only get weirder, my peace is interrupted. I try to remember that we call it "the present" because it's a gift.

In times of rapid change and uncertainty, we can become lost, uncertain of where we are, where to go, and what to do. At times like this, why not toss out all the old maps, find a safe, new home within yourself and follow your heart, which will guide you to what you most love to do?

The Buddhist teacher and life guide Joanna Macy writes,

> We are starved for beauty, so starved that we forget how important it is. We're in danger of losing our sense of what is authentic and true. I get nourishment from the night sky. I am also nourished by the beauty of the people whose lives encompass the natural world—who embrace an expanded definition of self-interest. People who risk their comfort, their material security, to try to slow down the destruction of the natural world inspire me.

I hope this book will empower you to work toward preserving life, in whatever way you can.

The Two-Thousands and Beyond: A New Radicalism Towards the Integral Paradigm

On September 11, 2001, in a near trance, I stared at the TV screen and watched the planes hit the towers—the burst of flames, the collapse. I watched over and over again, and then I sat down at my desk and wrote an email to a long list of colleagues, saying that this event, as horrible as it is, could serve as a traumatic wake-up call for Americans, requiring that we finally recognize that maintaining our way of life through a dependence on a diminishing stock of global resources is indeed unsustainable.

"Sustainability" was one of the big buzzwords of the 2000s, and not just in architecture. But how can we build more sustainably? Here in the U.S., unfortunately, government and special interests are a major part of the problem. Often, the folks that have the most to gain from a rule change are the ones who write it. Recently, California passed new rules for septic fields, rules that were written by the engineers whose business is to design and build them. The organization called Sightline.org documents regulations that prohibit common sense. In many suburbs, there are ordinances that prohibit drying clothes on an outdoor clothesline, and in one Michigan town a family was cited for growing vegetables on their front lawn. There, the local ordinance permits "only grass."

Most obstructive to ecologically intelligent design are the code barriers. These include the use of recycled materials, including straw bale and rammed earth, gray water reuse, composting toilets, and many new building-system products. (It took years to get approval for straw-bale construction and gray water reuse, which reuses 50 percent or more of household water.) Codes are necessary, but if we are going to design our way out of the mess we've created, codes must be conceived to allow for experimentation with new techniques and methods.

At a 2012 sustainability-policy summit in Santa Barbara, California, hosted by Oasis Design and attended by local officials and regulators from a number of California cities, host Art Ludwig laid out key issues to consider, including the following:

- The culture of regulators and policy makers is grounded in the belief that the current system delivers "the safest buildings in the world." Yet awareness of emerging risks due to climate chaos, toxics, and other causes is nearly nonexistent. While historical risks have dropped by about half in the last 40 years, emerging risks not covered by existing regulations have more than doubled.
- The action being taken to "green" buildings functions more as a diversion than a remedy. Industry interests have effectively captured large portions of the regulatory apparatus and are managing it for maximum profit.
- Unpermitted centers for research on sustainability in building and infrastructure have been the source of deep green innovation for years but their productivity is being dramatically lessened by tightening regulation, even as their innovation is needed more than ever.

The architecture business has become increasingly corporatized and largely serves those interests. In many cases, the production of construction drawings is outsourced to cheaper labor pools in India, Mexico, the

Philippines, and elsewhere. And for those who are just entering it, the future looks bleak. A *Washington Post* survey showed that recent graduates of architecture schools have the highest unemployment rate of fifteen college majors, at 14 percent. The lowest were in education and health, at 5 percent.

While the marketing of "sustainability", "green," and "Leadership in Energy and Environmental Design" (LEED) Gold medals is part of every office's pitch, many ignore the more basic questions of whether the design and uses for a new building are part of the solution or part of the problem. It's questionable how much impact the U.S. Green Building Council's popular LEED rating system has had on the reduction of fossil-fuel energy use in buildings, or how much it's reduced pollution and increased indoor air quality, because the system is based on design criteria and calculations rather than on measuring actual performance of a completed project. Until post-occupancy evaluation of actual building *performance* becomes the standard for learning from built examples, LEED appears as little more than a marketing tool. The USGBC needs to LEEP beyond LEED.

The International Living Building Challenge, developed by Jason McLennan of the Cascadia Green Building Council, is a major leap forward toward a more integrative, comprehensive, and inspiring approach to improving the art and science of designing and constructing built environments. The mission statement reminds us that, "we have only a few decades to reshape humanity's relationship to nature and bring our ecological footprint to within the planet's carrying capacity. Green progress is minute and barely recordable."

The Challenge addresses design related to site, water, energy, health, materials, equity, and BEAUTY (a dirty word in architecture), and it even includes spirit, inspiration, and educational value as criteria. Every project under consideration has to address a set of specific imperatives, with design solutions that demonstrate proven performance rates rather than anticipated outcomes. Urban agriculture, car-free living, biophilia, a human scale, rights to nature, ecological water flow, carbon footprint, and appropriate materials sourcing, construction, and removal are among them. Furthermore, the Challenge requires that 100 percent of a project's water come from rainwater or a closed loop; 100 percent of building energy must be produced on site; buildings must have operable windows; and materials must be supplied from within 500 miles.

While there has been much progress in terms of both awareness and action toward living and building more sustainably, we have a long way to go, in all sectors. And we can't overlook the fossil-fuel industries and their political power.

Of our total U.S. energy supply, the sun supplies less than 1 percent. Our best soils continue to erode from the production of corn and soybeans, most of which end up feeding animals and as major ingredients of junk food. The climate and resource clocks are ticking. It's a good time to recognize that the word "radical" means "root." We need to get to the root of the systems we've designed, the ones that are killing us.

"Transformation," Keynote, Cascadia Green Building Council, Seattle, WA, 2009

INTRODUCTION

The Transformation we are engaged in is transforming the world we now live in towards one that continues the gift of life to our future generations and all other forms of life with which we share this planet. For the first time in human history, what was always assumed as a certainty is no longer certain. The question is not saving the planet. The question is can we redesign human life to restore the planet's ability to support and sustain us? We all hear the continuous drum roll of depressing planetary news. Tonight I want to take you on a ramble through the landscape of our human story, some things I've learned, where we are now, what we can do, and what we can learn.

"The Great Turning" is a name for the essential adventure of our time: the shift from the industrial growth society to a life-sustaining civilization. I've been on this design journey for most of my life, bouncing along through hope, some accomplishments, and occasional despair as the question is always there, "Can we do it?" Forty years ago E.F. Schumacher gave us a useful answer:

Can we rely on it that a 'turning around' will be accomplished by enough people quickly enough to save the modern world? This question is often asked, but whatever answer is given to it will mislead. The answer "yes" would lead to complacency; the answer "no" to despair. It's desirable to leave these perplexities behind us and get down to work.

THE HUMAN STORY AND THE GREAT TURNING

… Studying human cultural history for many years …

THE ECO-LOGIC STORY

A few trends: ecosystems: fresh water, oceans, forests, soils, wetlands …

Energy:
16 trillion watts total global energy demand almost all from carbon sources … if we want

to cap carbon at 450 ppm by 2035 we will have to reduce to only 3 trillion watts from carbon (Stewart Brand: *Whole Earth Discipline*).

German Govt. says U.S. would have to be carbon neutral by 2020 to avoid worst climate chaos scenario.

Cities:
A billion people live in informal squatter cities mostly in developing world (op. cit. Brand).

Population:
Birth rate in developed world continuing to fall together with aging population.

Globally half of population is under 24, 85 percent in developing world.

Are we burning down the house of life to toast marshmallows?

THE THREE "R"s

Peter Calthorpe and I wrote one of the first books with the "S" word—*Sustainable Communities*—in 1986 (now back in print through New Society Publishers).

In the Introduction, I wrote,

> Sustainability is defined by its context. Sustainability implies that the use of energy and materials in an urban area be in balance with what the region can supply continuously through natural processes such as photosynthesis, biological decomposition, and the biochemical and natural ecological processes that support life. The immediate implications of this principle are a vastly reduced energy budget for cities, and a smaller, more compact urban pattern interspersed with productive areas to collect energy, grow crops, and recycle wastes.

That was an OK if naive beginning twenty-five years ago. My trusty 1993 *Random House Unabridged Dictionary* has no definition for either of the words "sustainable" or "sustainability," suggesting that even etymologists couldn't figure out what we were talking about. So I looked up how the dictionary defines "business" and it says, "The purchase and sale of goods in an attempt to make a profit." Then I happened to read that the Swedish word for "business" is "*nar lingings liv*" and it literally means "what supports life"! Yes, there's a world of difference between making a living and making a life.

"Saving the Planet," "Green," "Sustainable" are warm, fuzzy, terms without clearly shared meaning, values, and actions. What is meant by terms such as "Green" and "Sustainable" is far from transparent and too often becomes an excuse not to address fundamental issues. The use of the term "sustainability" gives us a false sense of security in that it implies that it is possible through technological change to design our way out of larger processes of ecological collapse and climate chaos.

The three "R"s for twenty-first century design are restoration, regeneration, and resiliency. This means integrating building design within a larger context of community design and the integral ecological design of food, water, energy, and recycling systems at every scale. Most of today's middle school students know the mantra, "materials cycle, energy flows, life webs." Today's designers need to imprint that mantra into their awareness.

The interactions among the natural world and the built environment on an urban, regional, and global scale are far too complex to lend themselves to simple metrics such as the term "sustainability" suggests. The problem with the word "sustainability" is similar to the problem with Wall Street's cunning phrase, "collaterized debt instruments." No one—including all the geniuses on Wall Street—knew what in hell they were buying and selling and a year later they still don't. As one Wall Street wizard quoted in a *New Yorker* article said, "So we trade chicken shit and call it 'chicken breasts.' No one knows the difference or really cares."

We know the big drivers—pollutants such as CO_2 and thousands of toxins in our soil, water, and bodies. We know climate has turned weird and unpredictable. We know remaining stocks of oil, gas, and coal have peaked and will have to be replaced with renewable energy from sun, wind, and biomass conversion. We know that the suburban dream is turning into a nightmare, that our infrastructure is rotting away, that in spite of the work of many good people, key ecosystems—forests, wetlands, good soils, fresh water, and ocean life—are endangered worldwide.

I used to rant to my Italian Swiss mechanic friend Rico about these issues; he sighed, rolled his eyes, and muttered something in his Valtellina dialect. "What did you say?" I asked. "It's an old observation from our region. 'People are like potatoes. They open their eyes only when they are up to their neck in shit.'" That colorful folk wisdom is an organic restatement of the fact that for a million years or more we have been wired only to respond to immediate physical threats. Comfort and denial take care of more distant threats.

We live in descriptions of reality, not reality itself. Jared Diamond's book *Collapse*, Charles Mann's *1491*, and Amy Chua's *Day of Empire* are recent works that tell the story of great societies throughout human history that collapsed because their rigid structures of belief could not adapt to new challenges, and through rigid denial overshot their ecological base.

Rigid structures—mental and physical—are unstable because they don't adapt easily to change. What we need to create are Resilient Communities. What does that mean? Quoting from my dictionary, "resilient" means "Spring back, rebound, the ability to return to the original form after having been compressed or stretched … recovery from illness, depression, adversity."

I've called it different things at different times but my lifetime belief has been that architecture is more than form and function. It's about the integration of all the elements that allow buildings to be what they are—organisms, and cities to be complex ecosystems. I was deeply influenced in architecture school in the fifties by becoming a member of the newly created Whole Systems Society that was trying to develop more wholistic approaches to the sciences. Bucky Fuller whom I studied with opened my eyes to design beyond the building envelope to consider all the forces that shape an environment without which neither buildings nor we can live.

What this means is that the design for a building or a city has to design for and integrate the flow of energy, water, waste, food, characteristics of land, place, culture, and history into its design. Organisms and ecosystems also change and evolve over time and that's also part of the equation.

I tested my ideas as "thought experiments" through my teaching, nonprofit institute and professional practice. The first was a 1971 Berkeley Architecture class where 15 students spent four days a week on a piece of wooded forest to design and build a core of buildings including an Ark—our meeting place, a cook house, a waterless privy, and individual sleeping places. We learned to forage local foods, scavenge native and used building materials, live with the ever changing forest, become aware of the precious value of basic resources. It was powerful learning for us all. One of the students, Rob Straus, wrote in our group publication entitled "Outlaw Building News":

> We will never know the experiments which discovered the order principles and integrities we carry in our genes. The genes have had

minds as their co-pilots. The purpose of minds is to help genes make life a success. Our failures are largely failures of the imagination. We know our image of things is wrong. We know this because things go wrong in our own image. If there is a global failure of life then it will be a failure in our own image, our image of living.

This first experiment taught me a powerful lesson in how we can coexist with nature in the wild in ways that are win-win. Since those days we've had the growth of what I call "eco-fundamentalism" which preaches nature is good, people are bad, and the two must be kept separate. The old environmentalist ideology preached saving natural systems from civilization. In building resiliency at all levels and scales the new environmental mission is integrating natural systems into our cities, communities, living places, and works places at every scale. Stewart Brand, in his challenging and brilliant new book *Whole Earth Discipline*, writes, "Accustomed to saving natural systems from civilization, Greens now have the unfamiliar task of saving civilization from a natural system—climate dynamics." I would add that what he calls "climate dynamics" is more accurately climate chaos—complex natural systems driven into insane chaos. In his classic *Mind and Nature*, Gregory Bateson makes the same analogy.

Next, we tried an urban experiment, buying an old house in West Berkeley because that's where the best soils are, having washed down from the hills over a century. We asked the question, "How self-reliant, resilient, and adaptable can we be on an urban lot? How much energy can we capture from the sun? How much food can we grow? How much rainwater can we catch, and how little water can we use? How little waste can we produce and can we recycle it back on the site?" Of course we understood we were located in a city and centralized systems were available to us to provide all our needs. We were not trying to be "Survivalists," just carry on experiments and keep careful records of the flows of energy, food, water, waste.

Fine Homebuilding, in 2006 in its twenty-fifth anniversary issue featuring the 25 most important homes built since Jamestown, included the Integral Urban House as "The Birth of Green." Now, as urban backyard gardens and chickens are making a comeback, our 1977 book *The Integral Urban House: Self-Reliant Living in the City* is once again a popular seller.

We moved up in scale from a forest village, to an urban lot, to a rural village, and then larger projects, each of which built on past learning and a belief that each project is a hypothesis to be tested and to learn from, and expand our understanding of whole systems that integrate the natural and the built environment.

Sustainability is static. Resiliency is dynamic. We are witnessing the collapse of large centralized systems from finance, the global food system, transport, the global fossil-fuel energy grid, the collapse of wild fisheries, shortages of fresh water, increasing regional wars over resources, and of course climate weirdness beyond our wildest nightmares.

For all these reasons, regions, major cities, small cities, towns, and rural areas need to redesign themselves with the goal of resiliency from the bottom up. Our urban skyscrapers can use transparent nano-solar cells to produce electricity and their walls and roofs to produce energy, grow food and sequester carbon, reclaim and recycle water. Parking lots can be turned into parks and sites to store run-off. Roof gardens everywhere. Literally green cities and towns. The New Ruralism will join with the New Urbanism to bring a greater level of resilience and awareness through food production in cities. Local energy and food and local economic self-sufficiency integrated with a fluid global economy. Leaping over LEED buildings to

LIVING BUILDINGS EVERYWHERE!!!

TRANSFORMING THE PRESENT

Eckhart Tolle in *A New Earth* writes,

> The greatest achievement of humanity is not its works of art, science, or technology, but the recognition of its own dysfunction, its own madness … To recognize one's own insanity is … the beginning of healing and transcendence … the ego is destined to dissolve and all its ossified structures whether they are institutions, corporations, or governments will disintegrate from within … The most rigid structures, the most impervious to change, will collapse first.

Design

Modern culture has thrived through the development of our left-brain capacity to reduce all problems to finite, rational solution algorithms. Yet, the design problems we face consist of multi-dimensional, complex systems issues that cross traditional disciplines and knowledge sets. We have to develop whole new mindsets, ways of working together, communicating across mindsets and tossing away old habits and inventing new collaborative processes to overcome today's fragmented, bunker mentality. We need to shift our focus on left brain to right brain, which is the basis for all design. We need to shift our focus from inter-disciplinary to "meta-disciplinary"—an integrated whole systems approach. You can't think out of the box. Thinking is the box.

- The upside down pyramid.
- Life Stories … If nature gets imprinted during childhood it endures throughout life. (How many renowned architects?)
- Whole New Mind: Agricultural Age, Industrial Age, Information Age (knowledge workers), Conceptual Age (creators and empathizers)
  – not just function but also DESIGN
  – not just argument but also STORY
  – not just focus but also SYMPHONY
  – not just logic but also EMPATHY
  – not just seriousness but PLAY
  – not just accumulation but also MEANING.

These six senses will increasingly guide our lives and shape our world.

- From obsession with metrics to pattern. (Alexander)
- LEEPing over LEED.

Environmentalists are accustomed to protecting natural systems from civilization. Now they have the unfamiliar task of saving civilization from dynamics of natural systems modern capitalism has driven insane—climate chaos.

CONCLUSION: YOU

The reality of a green world is here as we join in common purpose, climb out of our shells and join together. We have the knowledge, we have the power, we can create a livable future for the generations to come.

We all feel that change is coming, probably both good and bad in unexpected ways. Paul Hawken makes the case in his latest book, *Blessed Unrest*, that there are literally millions of groups all over the world working to regenerate their local economies and environments.

In times of rapid change and uncertainty, some people become lost, uncertain of where to go or what to do. At times like this, I suggest you toss out all your old maps and follow your heart to a new place within and do only what you love.

As Joanna Macy writes,

We are starved for beauty, so starved that we forget how important it is. We're in danger of losing our sense of what is authentic and true. I get nourishment from the night sky. I am also nourished by the beauty of the people whose lives encompass the natural world—who embrace an expanded definition of self-interest. People who risk their comfort, their material security, to try to slow down the destruction of the natural world and who take part in the evolution of a sustainable society inspire me.

> I tried so hard to find the route
> And found the route
> Is the root.
> …
>
> -live simply
> -laugh a lot
> -love deeply

Athena Award Reception Speech, Congress for the New Urbanism, San Francisco, CA, 2008

No two words are used more these days in our work than "sustainable" and "green."

In 1986, Peter Calthorpe and I wrote one of the first books with the "S" word: *Sustainable Communities*. In the Introduction, I wrote,

> Sustainability is defined by its context. Sustainability implies that the use of energy and materials in an urban area be in balance with what the region can supply continuously through natural processes such as photosynthesis, biological decomposition, and the biochemical processes that support life. The immediate implications of this principle are a vastly reduced energy budget for cities, and a smaller, more compact urban pattern interspersed with the productive areas to collect energy, grow crops, and recycle wastes.

That may have been a reasonable beginning twenty-two years ago, but our world was vastly different in those days. My 1993 *Random House Unabridged Dictionary* has no definition for either of the words "sustainable" or "sustainability." I looked up how the dictionary defines "business." It says, "The purchase and sale of goods in an attempt to make a profit." Contrast this to the Swedish word for business, "*nar lingings liv*," which translates as "what supports life." There is a world of difference between making a living and making a life. The interactions among the natural world, the world of money and commodification, and the built environment on an urban, regional, and global scale are far too complex to lend themselves to the simple metrics "sustainability" suggests.

We know the big drivers—atmospheric pollutants and carbon, the toxins in our soil, water, and our bodies. We know climate is turning chaotic, hotter, and increasingly unpredictable. We know remaining stocks of fossil fuels will have to be replaced with renewable, nonpolluting sources. We know the suburban dream of the 1950s has turned into a nightmare as our infrastructure rots away. In spite of the efforts of many good people, key ecosystems—forests, wetlands, good soils, fresh water, and ocean life—continue to deteriorate and disappear worldwide. When I started getting interested in relating design to ecology in the 1960s, the world population was 3.6 billion. Today it is close to 7 billion. I used to rant to my Italian Swiss mechanic Rico about these issues and human denial. He'd sigh, roll his eyes, and mutter something in his Valtellina dialect. "What did you say?" I'd ask. "It's an old observation from our region, 'People are like potatoes. They only open their eyes when they are up to their neck in shit.'" As the cultural historian William Irwin Thompson observed many years ago, "We live in descriptions of reality, not reality itself."

Eckhart Tolle in his book, *A New Earth*, writes,

> The greatest achievement of humanity is not its works of art, science, or technology, but the recognition of its own dysfunction, its own madness … To recognize one's own insanity is … the beginning of healing and transcendence … the ego is destined to dissolve and all its ossified structures whether they are institutions, corporations, or governments will disintegrate from within … The most rigid structures, the most impervious to change, will collapse first.

Rigid structures—mental and physical—are unstable because they don't adapt easily to change. What we need to create are "Resilient Communities." What does "resilient" mean? Quoting from my dictionary, "Spring back, rebound, the ability to return to the original form after having been compressed or stretched … recovering from illness, depression, adversity."

Sustainability is static, resilience is dynamic. Cities of all shapes and sizes, towns and villages, will all need to redesign themselves with the goal of resiliency. The walls of our urban skyscrapers will use transparent nano-solar cells to produce electricity, grow food, and sequester carbon. Parking lots can be turned into parks and store rainwater run-off. Roof gardens everywhere. Literally green cities and towns with local energy, food, and economic self-sufficiency integrated into a fluid global economy. I've coined the word "Surpassability" to suggest another process—one that begins with taking actions that move beyond the industrial/mechanical/anthropocentric/economic model which rules today. "Surpassability" implies thrival for all of human kind while "Sustainability" implies survival for only the richest in our global family.

What is needed is the emergence of a new world view where what we humans design and what evolution designs begin to merge and our minds evolve as part of a larger evolutionary process. Evolution is not blind as mechanists believe. We glimpse the possibilities of an ecologic world but, as yet, it has no distinct form physically or as social community. The danger at this time of turning is to try through our will to materialize what is still emergent. The ecologic world is within us waiting to find form. Once uncovered, it will emerge in its own way, its own time, in its own form.

We start with our most deeply held aspirations for ourselves and our world. Is this dream or fantasy? No, it's the new reality of a green world and it's doable now if we join in common purpose, leave our shell of denial, despair, and ego, and join together. We have the knowledge. We have the power. I hope we have the spirit, the story, the heart to create a livable future for generations to come.

So live simply, laugh a lot, and love deeply!

Keynote, Environmental Design Research Association, Sacramento, CA, 2007

In the next generation or two, we'll have to redesign most of what we've taken for granted during our lifetimes. To do that will mean that people will have to take the future into their own hands, not leave it up to the politicians, the corporations, and other existing powers. It's more than a design challenge. It means major changes in all our institutions—media, politics, commerce, and economics. None of our key institutions seem ready to meet the challenges we face.

We may be beginning to go through a profound shift in our global consciousness. In *Blessed Unrest*, Paul Hawken documents there are more than a million groups worldwide working locally to regenerate their environments. Cultural historians who follow the "Perennial Philosophy," which believes that humans evolve with the rest of nature, categorize human history in terms of our fundamental leaps forward through non-biological mutations called "cultural memes." The spiral of human evolution is like a strand of DNA moving through four-dimensional space/time. In a new world view, what we humans design and nature's evolutionary design begin to merge. Our minds evolve as part of a larger evolutionary process. The new paradigm will revolve around the regeneration and reassembly of the organic and its reintegration into the web of life.

What I discovered 30 years ago in managing California's design and building program is that most institutions have the design process backwards. We need to start with developing a basic mindset and mental model in which values, aspirations, and a shared world view sees us as part of an evolving nature. When we have a shared world view, different disciplines become an integrated team sharing a meta-discipline of design.

The most critical place to change a system lies not with metrics and numbers, but with challenging fundamental assumptions. We need to start with our most deeply held aspirations for ourselves and our world. In theologian/ecologist Thomas Berry's words, "We are ready for the New Story." The standard for ecological design, as David Orr puts it, is, "Neither efficiency or productivity, but health, beginning with the soil and extending through plants, animals and people." Ecological design is simply the effective adaptation and integration with nature's processes.

The compelling overall theme in the search for a unified approach to the design of systems—both built and natural—is integrating scales ranging from the molecular to the global. Industrial design, engineering, architecture, city and regional planning and infrastructure development can be woven together with the capacities and needs of specific bioregions.

This is a massive mind shift from the narrow world of the grid and lattice to the geometry of the fractal in which each part at every scale is a hologram of the whole. Nature's geometry is fractal at every scale from our galaxy to the geometry of air and water movement—from weather systems and currents, and the spiral whorl spinning down your shower drain. The nutrients, energy, and information essential to life, flow smoothly across scales ranging from micro-organisms to continents. By contrast, design has become fragmented into dozens of separate technical disciplines, each with its own specialized language and tools. If we are to include ecological concerns within design, we must find ways to integrate our design processes across multiple levels of scale. EcoDesign becomes the Meta-Discipline overriding the narrow mentality and obtuse language of separate scientific, technical, and design disciplines.

This year marks the tenth anniversary of the publication of *Ecological Design*. Our goal in writing the book is stated in the preface, "In order to successfully integrate ecology and design, we must mirror nature's deep interconnections in our own epistemology of design." In the book, we articulate five basic principles:

Solutions Grow from Place
The unique cultural and physical characteristics of place are often ignored by standardized designs. Our global economy works against knowledge and protection of place. Around the world, local groups are fighting to protect their cultural and natural heritage. The ecological, material, and human character of place are the true context of design, ignored by the mechanical commodification of life which creates a "geography of nowhere."

Ecological Accounting and Certification
We are developing successful voluntary rating systems to evaluate the human and physical consequences of completed design projects, including environmental and social factors of human use and resource flows affecting site, water, energy, materials, air quality, human health, and productivity. The goal of the most advanced system, the Living Building Challenge, requires zero net energy and water consumption, no CO_2, natural light, and locally sources building materials.

Design with Nature
This principle has found multiple expressions in the last ten years, ranging from Janine Benyus's groundbreaking book *BioMimicry: Innovation Inspired by Nature* to Robert Frenay's *Pulse: The Coming Age of Systems and Machines Inspired by Living Things*. Living systems have become a popular metaphor, model, and measure for the built environment, technologies, and social institutions such as the Internet.

Everyone Is A Designer
A new generation of designers places collaboration with all the stakeholders at the center of the design process. These include design teams that include clients, the building's targeted users, specialist consultants, regulators, and community members.

Making Nature Visible
All the evidence shows that when nature and its cycles are integrated into design, a building's users are more productive, more comfortable, and healthier. The concept is that of "biophilia." In an increasingly urbanized world, it is critical to make natural systems and natural processes visible and accessible to both children and adults.

In retrospect, perhaps the most compelling theme in *Ecological Design* is the search for a unified approach to the design of sustainable systems that integrates scales ranging from the molecular to the global. The last ten years have seen extraordinary theoretical and technical advances in the field of ecological design, while the challenges facing the planet have accelerated, ranging from the loss of biodiversity to the rapidly increasing impacts of global climate change, and the declining condition of dozens of ecosystem services providing clean water, healthy soil, and many others.

Frank Lloyd Wright once said, "The heart is the first feature of working minds." Nature's flows and cycles are integral to what we design and build. Our body, mind, breath, and heart are integral to our humanity. We can all move in the same direction healing our breach with ourselves and the living world and becoming more creative and happy in the process. Abraham Heschel reminds us, "We will not perish for want of information, but for lack of appreciation. What we lack is not a will to believe, but a will to wonder."

"Greening Campuses, Greening Education," Los Angeles, CA, 2006

My work life has been spent in education and architecture and what now is called "green," or "sustainable," design. When I started teaching at Berkeley as a 25-year-old professor, a wise mentor gave me advice that I have followed through a lifetime of teaching: "Teach what you most want to learn." What I most wanted to learn was how to design homes, communities, buildings, and cities that are more connected to the flows and cycles of the natural and living world, on which all life—including human life—depends. I taught and learned by designing a series of living–learning experiments in which classes designed and built increasingly more complex structures that connected built environments to the natural world. As we learned we scaled up, from a wilderness building-and-living experience to a model sustainable habitat; and then a real house, a rural village, state and university facilities, and the design for a new community of five thousand people.

We all know that the industrial era brought us a new way of life filled with new products and technologies, enriching our lives materially. We are less aware that the industrial era disconnected us from the impacts that our consumption and technologies have on our living world. While we gained materially, I believe we lost spiritually, as our lives became uncoupled from the primal evolutionary sources of life. Our life's journey needs to be more than absorbing information and mastering facts and skills.

In recent years, we come across the terms "green" and "sustainability" with increasing frequency—perhaps because more and more people and institutions recognize that the old industrial system no longer works. Let me try to explain what I think these terms mean.

"Green" refers to any technology or way of doing things that reduces the destruction of our environment and adds to what enlightened business calls "the triple bottom line," in which economy, ecology, and social equity all support each other. "Sustainability" is the multi-purpose term that refers to both the processes and end-state of realizing the mutual enhancement and overlapping of economy, ecology, and global equity.

My deepest love is for the natural world, which, since the Modern era, has largely been ignored by both architecture and education. Today we're meeting about green schools. So what are green schools? Green is the color of plants, from algae to trees. They're green because chlorophyll cells are essential to the photosynthetic process through which plants turn sunlight into carbohydrate, which is basically stored energy—fuel for humans and other organisms, or fuel for machines such as automobiles or the production of electricity. The biological meaning of *green* is what interests me in creating green architecture, especially in designing buildings for learning.

During the industrial era, the connection between the design and construction of buildings and nature's processes and ecology was lost. With the widespread adoption of air conditioning after World War II, and the development of a national freeway system, buildings lost connection to place. Air conditioning meant architects and engineers could ignore factors such as local climate and the orientation, size, and floor-plate dimensions of buildings, as well as the scale and context of existing buildings and communities.

After graduating architecture school, I worked in a respected architectural office that designed schools. The fashion at the time was to reduce windows to tiny fixed slits of glass at the corners of the classrooms and to install luminous ceilings providing high artificial even light levels with no shadows. The idea was that students would be less distracted from learning if there were no windows and that high, shadow-free artificial light levels improved learning. This experience convinced me that I could learn more by going into teaching than designing environments that considered young people as experimental rats in an architecture-education machine. Needless to say, their design assumptions were proven dead wrong.

Up until the 1970s electricity was so cheap, the cost of replacing daylight with electric light and the cost of cooling buildings with electricity rather than with properly oriented operable windows and other natural cooling devices were simply not considered. Mechanization took command over common sense or any sense of true human needs. A consequence of several generations of ignoring common-sense climate-responsive design is that the training of architects and engineers, for several generations, simply ignored time-tested natural climate design approaches. "Bioclimatics," learning how to design to reduce energy and resource use by understanding climate and natural environmental factors, didn't come back into architectural and building-engineering education until recently. Researching solar energy in the University of California library system during the late 1960s, I could find only two books on the subject, one published in the 1930s, one in the 1940s.

Freeways, cars, concrete, and mass-produced suburbs built with the other green (spelled: M-O-N-E-Y) in mind did the rest: destroying human and ecological communities and creating a "geography of nowhere." All of it was possible because of cheap and abundant energy. Flying from Palm Springs to Los Angeles, I see an uninterrupted swath of suburbs and strip malls for 100 miles or more. And then there's Las Vegas. As our grandchildren cope with the unsupportable mess we have created, I can hear them say, "What were you thinking back in those days?"

The two changes that will have the most severe impact on how we live are the fact that the world is running out of oil and oil is the lifeblood of our economy and way of life. The second major impact—the global climate meltdown it produces—follows from the first.

Carbon is the basic element of all fossil fuels—oil, coal, and natural gas. Every time you burn a gallon of gas in your car, you send 22 pounds of carbon dioxide gas into the upper atmosphere. If you drive 10,000 miles a year in a car with a fuel efficiency of 20 miles per gallon, you're contributing five tons to building a blanket of CO_2, which creates a warming effect in the upper atmosphere and, which we now know, destabilizes climate in known and unpredictable ways.

The U.S. Green Building Council's "Leadership in Energy and Environmental Design" (LEED) rating system is a good incentive to build more responsibly. It doesn't ensure that clients or their architects make the best strategic decisions or redesign the design process to fit new realities. I mentioned climate-responsive design as the most important single strategy to achieve more energy efficient, healthy buildings. The key concepts are simple: the orientation and the size and shape of the building is designed to follow the sun path—generally a narrow east–west oriented building is best because you can maximize sun on the south during the winter and control it during the hot months through external shading. Narrow buildings can use daylight and cross ventilation to replace expensive mechanical systems. Designing the building envelope for proper insulation and thermal transfer, or passive storage of heat or cool, is important. A study by the Rocky Mountain Institute shows paybacks of 1.5 to 4 years for such climate control measures.

In the 1990s, I designed the Solar Living Center, a green-products showroom and demonstration center in a Northern California valley with extremely hot summers and cold winters. Using principles I just mentioned, as well as largely recycled and reclaimed materials, we ended up with a building that has no heating or cooling system and only night lighting. It is a net exporter of energy into the grid from its solar electric system. It cost no more to build than a similar conventional building and has become such a popular destination for people to experience green technologies directly that they have created a school that offers a variety of hands-on courses in green technology and design. The building, built before LEED standards, received the American Institute of Architects' Top Ten Green Buildings Award in 1997, and if it were LEED rated, it would be Platinum Plus.

Beyond LEED, we can set the bar higher, towards "regenerative" or "living buildings" that go further than simply reducing resource and energy use but which produce all of their own energy, produce no CO_2 emissions, recycle all their water and wastes, incorporate some food production and green roofs in their buildings and site design, and go further than "carbon neutral" by absorbing CO_2 emissions from the surrounding environment. Regenerative buildings largely eliminate the need for expensive heating, ventilation, and air conditioning systems through design that fits climate, place, and site. By restoring natural systems to health and productivity, these buildings regenerate the sites where they are located. Regenerative buildings teach "eco-literacy." Every day, students and teachers and other end-users of the buildings would experience the connections and flows of human design and living systems. The walls separating subjects and disciplines dissolve so integrated learning can take place.

This brings up another issue that campuses that have been implementing green design and construction for a number of years have discovered: Green buildings don't automatically make sustainable campuses. The growing campus sustainability movement identifies a dozen other elements that need to be integrated into overall campus design systems and strategies in order to better achieve green goals. UC Berkeley's Campus Sustainability Committee includes nine campus-wide systems: energy, water, built environment, transportation, purchasing and waste, land use, food, health and well-being, academics and culture. These comprise 32 sustainability indicators of integrated campus performance. The report states, "A campus is more than simply an agglomeration of buildings … It is a combination of buildings, landscape features and surrounding context … LEED does not address this … use LEED as the foundation for a more holistic analysis of campus sustainability and long-term management."

The LEED rating system has played a key role in sparking a transformation in the design, construction, and real estate markets. The rating and assessment systems currently in use are proving effective at moving the building industry from conventional practice to a greener approach. It's a beginning but it cannot be an end; we have much further to go. While following its metrics slows the rate at which things get worse, it doesn't move us into the positive territory of regenerating and transforming the larger environment and our ways of thinking.

Mining platinum, gold, and silver ranks among the most ecologically destructive processes on Earth. To extract an ounce of gold, you have to rip up 30 tons of virgin soil and dose it with cyanide, and then the whole destroyed mess moves into watersheds, poisoning the soil and destroying aquatic systems. I like to kid my friends—David Gottfried, founder of USGBC and Rick Fedrizzi the CEO—that USGBC should honor LEED-rated buildings by naming them after species we're trying to save from extinction.

In April 2005, I attended an invitational conference sponsored by the U.S. Public Building Service, where two-dozen leaders in the green building field met to share their views on an expanding approach to green, having reached consensus that improving our technological fixes through tools such as LEED is not sufficient for the magnitude of change that will be needed for sustaining, restoring, or regenerating our communities and planet. Seven common themes emerged from the discussion:

1. Moving away from a totally human-centric view of the world.
2. Understanding the synergy between nature and human nature.
3. Appreciating the interconnectedness of the whole.
4. Using principles of living systems in our work.
5. Seeing ourselves as continual learners and avoiding hubris.
6. Encouraging dialogue and asking deeper questions, especially when they challenge accepted ways of thinking and doing.
7. Recognizing the role of spirit and love in everything we do.

Sustainability requires a shift in our mental models—a shift in thinking and in language, as most modern languages lack words to describe humans as an integral element in nature. I find the term "regenerative" useful because it suggests the self-healing, self-organizing, and self-evolving properties of living systems, which can co-evolve with design and designers grounded in natural-systems logic—what I call "eco-logic."

I can imagine that for many of you here—educators of architecture in a world of separate disciplines, or designers and builders dealing with hard cold technical realities—these thoughts from leaders in our field may seem unrealistic and airy-fairy. But ask yourself honestly: Are you working in a system that fails to ask the right questions or that fears fundamental change? Jared Diamond's latest wonderful book, *Collapse*, details (without judgment) what has happened to cultures throughout history when what they believe and how they act no longer fits ecological reality. Nature does bat last.

Let me leave you with a final thought: The world we live in today is changing in crucial ways that are challenging and frightening but full of positive opportunities. If we fear change, we respond through denial, escapism, and passivity. If we face change positively, with passion and hope, we just might realize our dreams of healthy buildings, healthy communities, and kids that are eco-literate and truly engaged in learning.

As a hopeless addict to dictionaries, let me tell you that the words "passion" and "passivity" come from the same Latin root: "to be moved by a higher force." The difference is whether the force to respond to chance comes from within or without. In passionate people, you can feel the "inner force" working to create positive change. On the other hand, passive people respond to what they experience as an outward force with passive acceptance: "You can't change the way it is."

You can feel change as a danger or an opportunity. You wouldn't be here today, if you didn't feel the opportunity to do good. I applaud each of you and the passion within you.

Further Reading: The Seminal Books of the Two-Thousands and Beyond

Urbanism in the Age of Climate Change
by Peter Calthorpe, 2010

Design Revolution: 100 Products that Empower People
by Emily Pilloton, 2009

World as Lover, World as Self: Courage for Global Justice and Ecological Renewal
by Joanna Macy, 2007

Collapse: How Societies Choose to Fail or Succeed
by Jared Diamond, 2004

The Nineties: Integrating the Ecologies of Nature, Culture, and Humans

In the 1990s, much of the positive momentum that had come to characterize the environmental movement of the 1970s returned and went mainstream; the radical ideas of the 1970s effectively watered down for a larger audience and clientele. The U.S. Green Building Council, founded in 1993, was about to become an important catalyst in promoting green and sustainable building, largely through its Leadership in Energy and Environmental Design (LEED) rating system. Still, post-occupancy evaluations of built environments—specifically their impact on human health and well-being and their performance (something I and a few others pioneered 50 years ago)—were ignored by the design professions.

The 1990s did, however, see opportunities to test innovative low-carbon building systems, including straw bale and rammed earth. In 1997, for a major green products company, we completed Real Goods Solar Living Center, a large and highly visible straw-bale project. In 1999, using rammed earth, waste materials from a nearby quarry, and reclaimed wood, we completed the Guitar House. The Life Expression Chiropractic Center in Pennsylvania, completed in 1998, was one of the first green-roof commercial buildings in the U.S. The materials and systems we used there also provided an opportunity to literally break out of the box and sculpt space with curves in all dimensions. (Nature has no straight lines, nor do our bodies.) Our improved analytic tools allowed more sophisticated analysis of site and building forms in relation to sun and climate. With that building, we moved into the second generation of ecological design—architecture that informed its users of the "story of place," told through the elements of sun, wind, earth, and water as they interact with the building.

During this period, most of our work was in natural places, helping people reconnect with nature. Experiencing the connections among the living and designed ecologies became an important part of our mission.

Overcoming the misconceptions of the role of design continued to be an uphill battle. Through our 1996 book, *Ecological Design*, Stuart Cowan and I were able to articulate for a wide audience both new ways to think about how and what we design and the human/nature connection. Nonetheless, the real problem, design education, remained. The problem with design education is that it starts too late. In most of our formal education, learning design skills and processes is limited to higher-learning professional programs in architecture and related skills, at the undergraduate and graduate levels. Beginning to learn how to design and how it can be an integrating tool for both human survival and our connection to the living world is elementary and thus ought to start in Grade 1.

In 1998, at the San Domenico School in San Anselmo, California, under the leadership of Sister Gervaise Valpey and working with Ecological Design Institute staff and with funding support by the Center for Ecoliteracy, we developed a program that integrated design and ecoliteracy at all levels of this K-12 private school. Third and fourth graders learned how to plan, create soil out of food waste from the school's cafeteria, and grow vegetables. Fifth to eighth graders participated in building tool-and-equipment sheds and, using straw-and-earth walls created from materials on site, a kitchen. They also carried out a solar analysis of existing school buildings. High school students did a professional-level ecological survey and mapping of the site, which covers a watershed. The attempts to use food waste from the cafeteria, which was then supplied by a major corporate food vendor, resulted in a drive to make the program entirely organic, using locally grown food. These initial efforts have spread throughout the school's curriculum and operations.

San Domenico was our first school garden project, and since then we have seen the movement grow exponentially. Analyzing the California K-12 math and science learning goals, we showed that they all could be achieved in a 100' by 100' school garden. Our motto became not "No child left behind," which is measured by the ability to repeat standard "right answers," but "no child left inside," which involves learning by doing, through direct involvement in living processes, including understanding how they work, interact, and can be designed, evaluated, and measured. It was one of the decade's important accomplishments.

Keynote, Solar Energy Association of Oregon, Twentieth Anniversary Conference, Portland, OR, 1999

Processes built on complex interlinked diversity is what sustainability is all about. We can apply the same criteria to guiding the future design of regions, cities, and buildings. From the overall principle of linked diversity we can develop design strategies for future urban and regional development that address each of the three "E"s: Economics, Ecology, and Equity. If we can do this clearly and comprehensively we may create a new ethics and a new esthetics for civilization into the next millennium.

Let's start with *Economics*. Conventional economics prices the value of land and materials made available by natural systems, but it does not price the value of services provided by these systems, such as providing clean air, purifying wastes, and water. Our present brand of industrial capitalism liquidates the common capital created by nature's evolution that we all share, and counts it as corporate income. In Paul Hawken's words, "Our present form of capitalism neglects to assign any value to the ecosystem services that make possible all life ... and also the social and cultural systems that are the basis for human capital." A team led by Stanford economist Gretchen Daly calculated that the ecosystem services flowing directly into society worldwide are worth at least $33 trillion, exceeding Gross World Product by 25 percent. In order to become truly sustainable, our present form of economics needs to wake up to ecological reality. As Hawken notes, "Many key ecosystem services have no known substitutes at any price." For example, the $250 million Biosphere II project in Arizona, which attempted to replicate specific ecosystems within a closed design environment, after a year's operation, was unable to provide breathable air for the eight "Bio-nauts" living within it.

Next, we consider *Ecology*. Let's consider everything that humans design and build as "Infrastructure." In this category, we include all buildings and services such as roads, communication and energy supply networks, and all technology that alters the given world of nature such as genetic engineering, agriculture, and industrial processes and production of all kinds. On the other side, is the design that our planet has evolved over four billion years: the biosphere, its biomes and ecosystems, and all the cycles, flows, and feedback processes that make it all work. Let's call that "Eco-structure." The design principle is to merge and overlap the natural and man-made systems through design that mimics how the natural world works. For example, we spend billions to design and build expensive, technologically complex sewage treatment plants to purify waste water and remove organic matter and toxic wastes. In nature, a marsh and wetlands can provide the same services without all the mechanics and engineering, just applying sound biological principles. We should be restoring wetlands which reduce flooding and also serve to purify waste water. Another obvious example is buildings. If we think about buildings as organisms rather than objects, then we design buildings that generate their own energy from the sun, reprocess their wastes, and use plant materials on walls and roofs to absorb carbon dioxide, produce oxygen, absorb rain and heat, and produce edible plants for food.

The last E is "*Equity.*" The principle is fairness and justice for all. No society is stable or sustainable when large numbers of its population are discriminated against economically and socially, without access to the education, housing, jobs, and other benefits available to mainstream society. When a society focuses on converting all values into commodities, community is the loser. If a neighbor brings dinner to a sick neighbor as an act of kindness, there is no upward tick in gross domestic product (GDP), but when a paid worker is sent to provide the same service, it adds to GDP. Money flow alone does not equal a healthy community. Redefining Progress, a San Francisco research group, developed an index that measures Quality of Life as compared to GDP. It shows a 45 percent decline in American quality of life since 1970, while GDP doubled. The major factor is that the increase in "progress" as measured in dollars, went mostly to the wealthiest 1 percent, while the middle class income declined.

Living fully in an increasingly complex technological world where every action and decision often affects far-removed living systems, requires a new form of literacy—ecological literacy. It requires cultivating what I call "ecological design intelligence"—a fluency in recognizing pattern, form, and relationship between the natural and the humanly designed worlds. It requires an understanding of past cultures and how they perceived and shaped their natural and built environments. Ecological design intelligence is more than understanding problems, it searches for and implements sustainable solutions that serve people and planet. Ecological design attempts to connect design efforts at different scales by building a common language that studies effects across scales of space and time.

Designers looking to natural systems to discover analogues useful in creating designed environments have an extremely large field of potential information to absorb. The book, *Biomimicry*, a book by Janine Benyus, provides a useful framework to study many examples at different scales in nature and their potential application in design at a variety of levels of scale. We are at the beginning of the learning curve, shifting the guiding metaphor from thinking of buildings as static machines or pieces of sculpture to conceptualizing them as dynamic living systems. In the nineteenth century, the English romantic John Ruskin declared that architecture was like frozen music, and the American architect Louis Sullivan prescribed that, "form follows function." Twenty-first century architecture may be guided more by the idea that, "form follows flow."

Nature's design is adaptive design. Ecologic design takes into account a wide timescale of adaptive strategies. Ecologic architecture adapts to people, place, and pulse. Traditionally, people, the eventual users and occupants of a building, are considered in the building program largely as a quantitative factor, rather than as a qualitative co-creator, inhabitant, and change agent of built form. Short-run, narrow focus economics tends to dominate the design program and design process.

In the era of globalization, which assumed cheap and abundant energy and materials, place seemed not to matter. Place has literally dematerialized. One place seems interchangeable with another. Architects and their clients have created a "geography of nowhere," often disregarding the physical and cultural context that makes one place unique from another. Each place has its unique ecological set of flows, cycles, and networks, physical and cultural, that create its character and qualities. The heart of ecologically intelligent design is to design with and for place. Better design begins by seeking answers to three fundamental questions about place. Good design begins, as Wendell Berry states, by asking, "What is here? What will nature permit us to do? What will nature help us to do here?" It requires careful observation, thoughtful questioning, and a measure of local genius and common sense. The answers to these questions will be reflected in buildings that are rich in regional integrity and character, places people can live well in place.

Next we turn to the concept of pulse. We start with a little known interesting fact. Regardless of size, each mammal lives for about 1.5×10^9 heartbeats. A shrew's heartbeat rate, or pulse, is many times that of a horse or a whale. Per unit of weight, it uses up many times more energy than larger mammals, it has a higher metabolism. We use "pulse" as a synonym for "metabolism"—the physical and chemical flows and cycles within an organism that maintain life. All materials, systems, also cultures are entrained in complex temporal and spatial pulses. This suggests several principles in designing buildings that fit their environments. Think of buildings as humanly designed ecological systems. Try to diagram and measure their metabolism —the input, conversion, and output of energy and materials. Optimize their ecological footprint—the impact and interactions of their metabolism with other systems.

Thinking about humanly designed systems as analogous to living systems in terms of metabolism is a new form of thinking. It is critical in a world where our decisions about the morphology of humanly designed systems have profound consequences for the living systems in which they are embedded. In the generation since sustainability first became a design criterion, the tendency has been to focus on measuring the energy and material flows that result from resource extraction. "Picking the low hanging fruit" was an effective initial strategy. Now we have to shift our focus to the far more difficult task of accounting for natural capital for which no technological substitutes exist, and which are far more difficult to measure.

Lastly, let's consider three important strategies to reduce a building's design metabolism: integrated life cycle costing, de-carbonization, and dematerialization. Integrated life cycle costing establishes the value of the building over time as a whole and all its particular components. Integrating mechanical systems with natural systems— such as daylighting plus artificial lighting, or natural ventilation plus mechanical ventilation—may be one way to extend useful life and reduce metabolism. De-carbonizing buildings includes both reducing carbon outputs and also designing the building to absorb carbon through green walls that absorb CO_2 and excess heat. De-carbonizing strategies, including street trees and tree-filled parks, give true meaning to "greening" the city. Dematerialization means doing more with less by substituting design intelligence for brute force and stuff. We have come a long way in dematerialization through technology. Design has its share of visionaries, such as Buckminster Fuller, preaching better design through more efficient use of materials, miniaturization, and studying nature's solutions. The search will continue.

KEYNOTE, SEAO, PORTLAND, OR, 1999

"Healthy Building," *Resurgence*, March–April 1993

> In the beginner's mind there are many possibilities, but in the expert's there are few … The real secret of the arts: always be a beginner.
> —Shunryu Suzuki, *Zen Mind, Beginner's Mind*

Suzuki Roshi used to say that Zen practice requires the quality of beginner's mind, experiencing everything for the first time, fresh. One of the key processes is "dwelling," which is our relationship with the built environment. Let's recall that "health" derives from the Indo-European root, "haele," to be or to make whole. To restore health, in the deepest sense, we need to find new forms of wholeness in our building and dwelling.

Looking at the contemporary landscape with beginner's mind can be harrowing: this should be a strong clue to our present predicament. Too much architectural practice has devolved into the replication of lifeless, abstract models. These standard patterns of land use, building types, roads, and infrastructure may be termed "templates," for they are mechanically traced from the abstractions of economics, planning, and building codes. They are part of a largely unexamined epistemology and consciousness which is reproduced through culture, education, and professional indoctrination.

Despite the mantle of sophistication surrounding design, in many ways we are lost about fundamental values and what counts for knowledge. In the 1990s, ecology and conviviality are finally returning to the architectural scene; let us celebrate this new flowering. We need to rethink what we are doing and the spirit in which design is undertaken.

The *industrialized world* with its science, technology, and borrowed affluence, developed by denying wholeness within the art of living. In *Mechanization Takes Command*, the architectural historian Siegfried Giedion painstakingly documents how the modern American city catalyzed a series of technological "advances" and facilitated the mechanical disassembly of living forms. Growing nineteenth-century urban populations displaced from the land by capitalism and the factory system needed large quantities of cheap food. The invention of the mechanical reaper made possible the large-scale cultivation and harvesting of grains. Later Pillsbury invented the technology to separate the wheat germ from the whole grain, giving the new city dwellers white bread impervious to quick spoilage. Cheap grains triggered an explosion in the number of livestock, which led to the first modern assembly line, designed to kill and dismember hogs. It featured a moving overhead line where carcasses were disassembled. Each worker performed a specific, carefully programmed operation. A young engineer by the name of Henry Ford visited one of these meat plants, and the modern auto assembly line was born soon after.

In a very literal way, the mechanical dis-assembly of life was joined to the mechanical re-assembly of machines, buildings, and soon the whole environment. Wholeness—given its notorious elusiveness, incapable of reduction or measurement—is considered simply an indefinable romantic or spiritual notion not worthy of consideration by practical men and women of the world. Without wholeness, we are left only with fragments of knowledge, fragments of life.

It is clear that design and technology since the Industrial Revolution have been about disassembling organic nature. Now we need to heal, to make whole. The work before us is to recreate and regenerate natural systems through our designs. Designs which are integrally connected to nature can profoundly influence human consciousness and well-being. By listening more carefully to beginner's mind in the integral design process, we provide seeds for a more integral consciousness, one that is attuned to wholeness and health in myriad ways. To attempt to design a shift in consciousness would be foolhardy; we can only hope the shift will be catalyzed by a more convivial environment.

As an entry to beginner's mind, we offer five principles to reshape the environments we create towards health and wholeness. They may be applied at all levels of design scales, from doorknobs to cities. After all, beginner's mind cannot define its own boundaries and therefore won't experience them.

1ST PRINCIPLE: DESIGN WITH LITTLE "N" NATURE

Big "N" Nature is the natural world conceived as "out there" in remote mountain ranges, in rainforests, and what we call "wilderness." Too often we believe that our own activities can be carried out without harming Nature's processes. Healthy design can bring an elemental awareness of natural processes and interactions into even the urban context. Designing with little "n" nature means making natural processes visible and active in very ordinary ways at levels of scale from the household to the neighborhood to the entire city. Presently, the reflected light of cities hides the night sky, underground drains hide rainwater courses, and distant landfills hide cycles of biological decay and renewal. Our challenge is to make long hidden processes both visible and viable.

Unless we weave little "n" nature back into the everyday environment, big "N" Nature will become an expendable abstraction confined to television documentaries. Our daily lives need to be intimately connected to natural cycles. When we come to experience and participate in organic processes as a necessary and intimate part of our lives, the awareness and motivation to protect the larger natural systems, Nature, will be widespread and enormously powerful. The contemporary abyss separating nature and culture is a relatively recent pathology. Design with little "n" nature will help reweave nature and culture, regenerating both.

2ND PRINCIPLE: DESIGN ECOTONES

An ecotone is a place where two or more ecosystems meet. For example, in San Francisco Bay, fresh water from the Sacramento and San Joaquin rivers flowing from the mountains meets the salt water of the Pacific, providing an extraordinary range of habitats. Ecologists have long recognized ecotones as places of high biodiversity and great fertility. Other examples include wetlands where tidal waters flow in and out of marshlands and where forests open up to meadows. An ecotone is a soft overlapping of very different ecologies. Ecotones are

highly permeable; they are the opposite of a hard edge or boundary which presents a barrier to the flow of resources, energy, or information. Ecotones apply both to natural systems as well as human social diversity.

Most design ignores ecotones. City planning practice as it developed in the early twentieth century emphasized zoning new development into single use land zones for housing, industry, commerce, and recreation. The older, more organic concept of mixed uses in close proximity was discouraged. Architects focused on creating new prototypes of single use buildings which inevitably neglected edges and interfaces with other systems both natural and human. Architects are still designing the "it" and seldom the edge, even though it is at the edges or ecotones where exchanges and interactions take place.

Planning and development favor clear separation between land uses, while the automobile eats ecotones and turns them into dead zones. Thus we are left with the sterile empty plazas, parking lots, and highway edges of much new development. The designed ecotone can promote contact between people and natural systems. Other ecotones are simply accidental, or occur organically. The "town–gown" edge where campuses meet the local community is one example. Grandiose urban renewal schemes often sweep away such vibrant places.

Designers could study three carefully cultivated ecotones that have evolved over millennia: the garden, the village, and the diversified family farm. Each incorporates a complex set of interfaces between people and nature. These forms have been around so long and have worked so well as ecological designs that they can continue to teach integral designers.

3RD PRINCIPLE: SUSTAINABILITY IS CONSERVATION PLUS REGENERATION

"Sustainability" is bandied about a great deal, often without a very deep consideration of what it might mean. Clearly, sustainability implies conservation of matter and energy so that future generations may prosper. Yet attention to conservation is not enough; we also need to regenerate human and non-human life. Design for conservation is in the realm of efficiency: harnessing renewable energy, reducing water usage, recycling. However, conservation alone will hardly guarantee wholeness. Regeneration attempts to bring back life to creeks, marshes, cities. It increases syntropy rather than decreasing entropy. Design for regeneration is in the realm of health. Designing for regeneration will create spaces which foster rather than hinder conviviality. As we regain our ability to dwell well, it will enrich design practice.

4TH PRINCIPLE: USE THE ORGANIC METAPHOR ACTIVELY

Non-industrial cultures conceive of buildings as alive, giving them a sacred quality. In contract, our mechanical paradigm reduces buildings and environments to machines to live and work in. Now a new synthesis of biology and design encourages us to actively use the organic metaphor. When I went to architectural school, we learned to fashion building walls like static painting. Now we can design building walls that can respond to the human skin, to changing atmospheric and thermal conditions. Inventions such as low emissivity glass and cloud gel spring from the vision of buildings as living, breathing organisms not unlike our own bodies. The harsh walls of industrial design are softened by biological membranes.

John and Nancy Todd and their associates at the New Alchemy Institute on Cape Cod reason that to create a healthy and productive living environment, its composition should mimic that of our planet. Their self-sustaining "Arks" on Cape Cod and Prince Edward Island were designed to encompass 30 percent terrestrial habitat and 70 percent aquatic, mirroring the planet ratio. This principle helped foster a richly composed ecological environment that can exist even through long, cold winters.

Living system buildings allow us to move from efficiency to health and wholeness. They clean air, grow food, calm the spirit. When designing with living processes, instead of ignoring them, a new realm of esthetics is opened up, and perhaps evolving a new ethics.

5TH PRINCIPLE: ALIVENESS AND WHOLENESS

The Dogon people of West Africa and many other earlier cultures conceive of their houses as a body with each part having corresponding function as the human body. In children's art, we experience the aliveness that children experience as they create. When we become one with what we create, it embodies our aliveness. Many of us have experienced this "flow state"—those moments when there is time and the voice of reason in our head is no longer judging us. Many buildings and planned communities built in recent times give me the feeling that no one was home when they were designed. They feel like they were designed and built by machines: no one home. Their designers were responding to "design constraints," not the needs of living people. Since every environment we design becomes home to someone, if there is no one home in the design process, the result may be an environment that can never be home to anyone.

An environment that is alive has a voice. With a voice, there can be resonance and dialogue between building and inhabitant. Whenever a building or environment is deeply alive, it can enhance the wholeness of all living beings who come in contact with it.

The five principles I've discussed are only a few ways of translating ecological understanding into design. Designers have a role in the evolution of our understanding of natural process which cannot be the exclusive domain of science. Fields and phenomena are merging and the old boundaries that used to be hermetically sealed disciplines from each other are dissolving. Where there were once unitary perspectives, there are now multiple, complementary perspectives.

In the old biological thinking, organisms played out their Darwinian rites against a static environment. In the Gaian paradigm, the whole biosphere is in grand polyphonic communication with itself. Living organisms co-evolving with their environment adjust everything from the composition of the atmosphere to the salinity of the oceans. Together with the competitive evolution of organisms is the cooperative co-evolution of species, dancing together to find mutually supportive niches. Co-evolution suggests that the old epistemology, which considers organism and environment as separate, does not give us a good picture of natural process. Organism and environment form a single entity, co-evolving together. For example, consider species such as the California condor whose natural habitat is gone. The remaining condors live in zoos, raised from eggs lifted from native nests. Without their habitat is the zoo condor truly a condor? The old biology tells us organisms adapt to changes in their environment, but the new picture is rather more ambiguous.

A dance teacher told me that in her twenty-five years of teaching, she has noticed that as the pace of life has speeded up, her students have become less coordinated in their movements. As we become less coordinated, are we in danger of passively accepting an environment that uses less of our natural kinesthetic and sensory potential? Designers co-evolve with their work. When we create environments that are truly alive and whole, it makes us, and everyone who participates in what we create, more alive and whole.

Emergence is a powerful metaphor for the kind of transition facing designers. It is defined as the extraordinary leap from one world to another. There is emergence in the coordination of billions of neurons to engender the thoughts and intuitions that shape a building. There is emergence in human culture and cities, in ecosystems and economics. It is likely that human consciousness has not completed its emergence. An integral state of consciousness is emerging, but not in a clear, linear fashion, but out of crisis and chaos. As we attempt to foster health during this difficult transitional time, we can expect powerful synergies along the way. We can honor the immediacy of beginner's mind, and once again trust our most intimate experiences as measures of the viability of our environment.

Keynote, First Los Angeles Ecological Cities Conference, University of California, Los Angeles, 1991

Sustainability borrows from observing biological systems. What nature does to combat instability in a particular environment evolves an integrated or linked diversity in which many species, at all scales, are connected through flows and cycles. Rivers are designed to flood without doing harm. Their banks are lined with trees that prevent erosion. Their immediate low-lying areas or flood plains are populated with plants and animals adapted to thrive on occasional floods. Those places where two kinds of natural systems come together—for example, where forest meets grassland or where tidal waters meet land—are called *ecotones*, and they are typically places of maximum biological diversity and productivity, and they are constantly changing yet maintain relative stability. Processes built upon a complex interlinked diversity—that's what sustainability is all about. We can apply the same criteria to guiding the future design of buildings and cities.

From this overall principle of linked diversity, we can articulate design principles and strategy for each of the three "E"s: Ecology, Economy, and Equity. Through the application of principles and strategies, we can create a new ethics and a new esthetics for civilization into the next millennium.

Let's start with the design of economics. Conventional economics prices the value of land and other materials made available by natural systems, but it does not price the value of services provided by these systems, such as providing breathable air, purifying wastes, and water. Our present brand of industrial capitalism liquidates its capital and calls it "income." In Paul Hawken's words, "Our present form of capitalism neglects to assign any value to the ecosystem services that make possible all life … and also the social and cultural systems that are the basis for human capital." Just to make the point, a team led by a Stanford economist calculated that the ecosystem services flowing directly into society worldwide are worth at least $33 trillion, exceeding Gross World Product by 25 percent. In order to become sustainable, our present form of economics needs to wake up to ecological realities. As Hawken notes, "many key ecosystem services have no known substitutes at any price." For example, the $250 million Biosphere II project in Arizona, which attempted to replicate ecosystem functions within a closed designed environment, was unable to provide breathable air for the eight people living within it.

Next, let's consider ecology and design. Let's consider everything that humans design as infrastructure. That includes all buildings, services such as roads, communication, and all technology that alters the given world of nature, such as genetic

engineering, agriculture, and industrial processes. On the other side is the design that the planet has evolved over four billion years: the biosphere, its ecosystems, and all the cycles, flows, and feedback processes that make it all work. We can call that "eco-structure." The design principle is to make the two work together, through the design of infrastructure that mimics how the natural world works. For example, we spend billions to design and build sewage treatment plants that remove organic matter from waste water. Yet this is precisely what a marsh does. We should be restoring wetlands, which reduce flooding and also serve to purify waste water, at costs far lower than conventional sewage treatment plants. Another obvious example is buildings. If we think about buildings as organisms rather than objects, then we design buildings that generate their own energy from the sun on-site, reprocess their wastes, and use plant materials on walls and roof to absorb carbon dioxide and pump out oxygen.

The last E is "Equity." Here the principle is simply that of fairness and justice. No society is stable or sustainable when large numbers of its members are left out of the mainstream, absorbing all the hits and none of the benefits.

Globally and regionally, the focus on turning all values into monetized commodity is the enemy of maintaining community. Money flow does not equal healthy community. Redefining Progress, a San Francisco research group, has developed an index that measures Quality of Life as compared to GDP. What it shows nationally is a 45 percent decline in quality of life since 1970, while GDP doubled. One economic design solution is to begin to use local currencies—banks where people exchange services rather than paying cash for them. In Switzerland, 86,000 people belong to a local currency system ("LETS"), encouraging more personal exchange and a sense of community.

BUILDING ECOLOGY: PLACE, PEOPLE, AND PULSE

The building and construction sector uses more energy, materials, and land than any other sector of human activity. If we are going to reverse the present alarming decline in the health of the planetary environment, changes in how, what, and why we build play a key role in determining the human and planetary future.

The five principles of ecological design are:

1. The best solutions start from paying attention to the unique qualities of place.
2. Trace the direct and indirect environmental costs of design decisions using environmental accounting.
3. Mimic nature's processes in design, so that your design fits nature.
4. Honor every voice in the design process.
5. Making nature visible through design transforms both makers and users.

Designers looking to natural systems to discover analogues useful in the design of the built environment have an extremely large field of potential information to absorb. In my field, architecture and design, we are only at the beginning of the learning curve, shifting the guiding metaphor from thinking of buildings as static machines or pieces of sculpture to conceptualizing them as dynamical living systems that are the very nature of nature. In the nineteenth century, the English Romantic writer John Ruskin declared that architecture was like frozen music, while the American architect Louis Sullivan prescribed that form follows function. Twenty-first-century architectural design may be guided more by the ideas that architecture *is* music and form follows flow.

Nature's design is adaptive design. At the long timescale, design for adaptation equals evolution; at the short timescale, adaptation is ad hoc innovation and change. Ecologic building design takes into account a wide timescale of adaptive strategies and scenarios involving place, people, and pulse.

I propose that architecture respond to these three key shapers of form, each of which is largely ignored by today's architects. Most contemporary buildings are shaped by the abstract short-run economic programs of corporate and institutional clients and by the fashion dictates of their architects. People, the eventual users and occupants of a building, enter most building programs only as a quantitative factor, not as a qualitative co-creator, inhabitant, and change agent of built form. Short-run, narrow-focus economics dominates the design program and design process.

The goal in ecological design is to create buildings and environments that are "ecomorphic;" that is, their internal structure mimics and integrates with the natural systems within which they are embedded and connected. Ecomorphism means something different than an architectural form being derived directly from nature, such as a bridge's structure resembling the structure of a bird wing, or a house looking like a nautilus shell. These are examples of "biomorphism"—forms taken directly from nature. Ecomorphism goes deeper, implying architectural processes and forms at many scales adapted to nature.

In the era of globalization and cheap and abundant energy and materials, place seems not to matter. Place has literally dematerialized. One place seems interchangeable with another. If we found ourselves in the downtown of any large city in the world, we would know we were downtown somewhere, but where?

Community is a much overused and imprecise word. *Place*, on the other hand, implies all those ecological connections, flows, cycles, and networks, cultural as well as physical, that give a geographic location its character and qualities. A biome is a particular community and so is an ecosystem. The heart of ecologically intelligent design is to design with and for place.

Better design begins by seeking answers to three fundamental questions about place. Good design begins, as Wendell Berry stated, by asking, "What is here? What will nature permit us to do here? What will nature help us do here?" It requires careful observation, thoughtful questioning, and a measure of local genius and common sense. The answers to these questions will be reflected in buildings that are rich in regional integrity and character, in built environments where people can live well in place.

To understand the problem, you need to understand how most buildings built for large organizations get designed, whether they are public, private, or nonprofit sector. Someone is in charge of facilities, meaning buildings. They generally are charged with getting the most square footage for the least money. The requirements for the new project are generally communicated to the architect in a "building program" and a budget. The building program is generally a thick book listing all the required spaces the building must contain as well as other standards that need to be met in the design. The budget sets a dollar number for the project cost. Significantly, it does not contain a budget for operations and for maintenance.

Usually the program omits any specific goals for the building's performance in either material or human terms. In the typical organization, personnel represent 92 percent of total costs; buildings, including first and operating costs, only 8 percent. Yet few organizations attempt to connect the design of a facility to the desired outcomes in terms of the building's use. Does one type of school facility produce better results than another type? Does one office facility result in lower absenteeism than

another? How does the design of a healthcare facility enhance or deter recuperation from illness? How do particular environments promote health and well-being while others promote ill-health and unease? One would expect that the large investments in facilities would be guided by the answers to questions that relate people's behavior to a particular designed environment. For example, is the typical windowless office "cubicle farm"—the subject of a thousand Dilbert cartoons—the most cost-effective corporate work environment or simply the result of lazy, uninformed design? In the Netherlands and Germany, based on health and productivity studies, labor law requires that a workstation be no more than seven meters from an operable window. Recent studies of school and retail environments document 26 percent improvement in learning and 40 percent sales increases in daylight spaces.

Lacking a scientific basis to plan for people's needs, preferences, and aversions in buildings, the next best thing is to have people participate directly in planning their buildings and environments through intensive interactive workshops known as "charrettes." The charrette roughly approximates a project's human ecology by including a sample of all the stakeholders in the group.

Not only do poorly designed buildings threaten the environment and communities, human health and happiness are also under threat. The physical and psychological needs of people have been reduced to a narrow band of physical parameters, and performance is measured by the bottom line. The question most often raised regarding green buildings is whether the incrementally higher first cost of a building incorporating eco-logic is worth it in terms of tangible human benefits, particularly as measured in enhanced performance. We have forgotten that the places we live and work in influence the flow of ideas, the quality of learning, and the human relationships of their occupants. The process of design is an opportunity for a community to deliberate over the ideas and ideals it wishes to express and how these are rendered into architectural form. What do we want our buildings and communities to say about us? What do we want them to say about our ecological prospects?

PULSE: METABOLISM AND FLOW

We start with a little-known interesting fact: Regardless of size, every mammal lives for about 1.5 billion heartbeats. However, a shrew's heartbeat rate, or pulse, is many times that of a horse or a whale. Per unit of weight, it uses up many times more energy than larger mammals; it has a higher metabolism. We use "pulse" as a synonym for "metabolism"—the physical and chemical flows and cycles within an organism that maintain life. All materials, systems, and also cultures are entrained in complex temporal and spatial pulses. This suggests several principles in designing buildings that fit their environment. First, think of buildings as humanly designed ecological systems. Second, diagram and, if possible, measure their metabolism—the input, conversion, and output of energy and materials. Third, optimize their "ecological footprint"—the impacts and interactions of their metabolism on other systems.

Thinking about humanly designed systems as analogous to living systems in terms of metabolism is a radically new form of thinking, yet it is critical in a world where our decisions about the form and shape, or morphology, of every humanly designed object and system have profound consequences for the living systems in which they are embedded.

Let's take a familiar example: The typical home. Before the home was built, its site may have been a forest, grassland, farmland, or wetland, each with its own metabolic flows converting solar energy to biomass, absorbing carbon dioxide and producing oxygen, and providing habitat for a myriad of small creatures, each with their own metabolic cycles. All of these are altered by the act of building. To construct the house, trees are cut in far off locations, metals refined, plastics manufactured. Each building material has its own metabolic cycle that interacts with natural systems. When the house is completed and occupied, a new set of cycles comes into play. Gas, oil, or electricity is burned to heat, cool, and light the house. The output is waste heat and carbon dioxide, dumped into the surrounding atmosphere. The occupants travel from and to the house by car, again burning fuel. Food grown in far-off locations is purchased and consumed, with the wastes disposed in landfills. Clean water is brought in and discharged together with human wastes and other water-borne debris.

Multiply the single home by tens of millions, and we find that the metabolic flows arising from human design decisions and the living patterns they produce have a huge effect on the metabolism of natural systems at a planetary scale. Ecologic design connects specific design decisions to their impacts on natural systems and through that process generates very different design decisions and very different design solutions. Consider the simple example of the new home that is ecologically designed. It will not be built of virgin wood but of materials reclaimed and remanufactured from the waste stream. Its energy demand will be reduced through climate-responsive design and energy-efficient equipment. It may produce part of its energy from the ambient environment. It will recycle its water and wastes, and occupants may eat lower off the food chain or grow some of their own foods. The neighborhood and community pattern will be designed to reduce automobile use.

The different players in this design drama—land developers, local government agencies, material producers, builders, and consumers—are probably unaware of the metabolic chaos their decisions unleash. It's not part of their decision or design process. They don't know or share the concepts and language that would allow them to behave differently. And so what the ecologist Garrett Hardin called "the tragedy of the commons" unfolds, step by unwitting step.

We are only in the first stages of being able to translate ecologic thinking into design tools that allow us to trace metabolic effects through the system. Today, there are not many incentives for doing so, since government regulations and our economic system tend to ignore the relationship between self-interest and common interest; the relationships among three types of capital: financial, human, and natural capital.

Intelligent design decision-making needs to take into account the complex interaction of all three forms of capital. The three are not commensurable, and they operate on different time and space scales. Here science can help us. Faced with complex phenomena, science turns to reductionism, analyzing small pieces for clues as to how the whole interacts.

This leads us to an emerging conceptual tool in the development of ecologic design practice: ecologic footprint. An ecologic footprint is an accounting of the resource flow and ecosystem services required to bring a particular design product or system into being, whether it be a square yard of carpet, a genetically engineered tomato, a new home, office building, or the sum total consumption of a median American lifestyle. A yard of synthetic carpet requires electrical or heat energy in its manufacture. It requires water, and it requires hydrocarbon feedstocks from virgin or recycled sources. Its manufacture produces heat, carbon dioxide, waste water, and fiber waste. Computed

per yard, these various inputs and outputs equal the carpet's metabolism, or footprint.

Mathis Wackernagel and his colleagues have calculated the ecologic footprint per capita of selected countries in terms of the amount of forest land, cropland, and grassland required to sequester carbon, grow food and fiber, and sequester wastes. This provides a baseline to determine how many people the planet can support at a particular level of affluence and technology. For example, if the entire world population lived at a North American level of consumption, it would take the ecosystems of two Earths to take care of basic functions like food, fiber, and carbon sequestration. The footprint concept offers a promising method of translating the complexities of design metabolism into a resource and ecosystem language and a currency that people can understand and use in evaluating design and consumption choices.

In the generation since sustainability first became a design criteria, the tendency has been to focus on easier to measure energy-and-material flows that result from resource extraction. "Picking the low-hanging fruit" was an effective initial strategy. Now we have to shift our focus to the far more difficult task of accounting for natural capital for which no technological substitutes exist, and which are far more difficult to measure.

When we begin to design buildings from the point of view of metabolism and pulse, we move to three important strategies: integrated life cycle costing, de-carbonization, and dematerialization. Integrated life cycle costing establishes the value of the building over time, both as a whole and also for its particular components. Replacing movable furnishings does not seriously interrupt a building's use, while replacing a heating, ventilation, and air conditioning (HVAC) system does. Integrating mechanical systems with natural systems—such as daylighting plus artificial lighting, or natural ventilation plus mechanical ventilation—may be one way to design redundancy in our buildings, extending useful life and reducing metabolism.

Reducing the throughput of carbon in buildings is critical to coping with the growing problem of global warming. The obvious measures include energy efficiency and climate-responsive design. The latter, if taken seriously, would have the effect of outlawing our current "big box" building footprints, which cannot function without massive energy-intensive HVAC and lighting systems. Less obvious and more intriguing is to design buildings with built-in carbon sinks such as a second skin of living materials that absorb carbon dioxide and other toxins. As 30- and 40-year-old glass and metal walls wear out, they can be replaced with a double skin of energy-producing, heat-absorbing, high-performance glazing and an outer skin of carbon-dioxide-absorbing plants. As parts of the urban fabric wear out, they could be replaced with forests. De-carbonizing strategies such as these would give true meaning to "greening the city."

Dematerialization—doing more with less by substituting design intelligence for brute force and stuff—has been around a long time. One need only read a book such as *Undaunted Courage*, Stephen Ambrose's account of the 1803 Lewis and Clark expedition, to comprehend how far we have come. As Ambrose points out, at the time of the expedition the speed of human travel had not advanced in thousands of years, since the domestication of the horse. The Pony Express took weeks to carry a message across country and at a great material cost. Now travel and communication have not only speeded up almost infinitely, they require vastly fewer resources per unit of service. Ambrose tells us of the thousand pounds of equipment required by the explorers to locate their geographic position in latitude and longitude. Now we can pinpoint our location through the use of global positioning system (GPS) handheld equipment weighing a few ounces. Per-unit computing power has fallen from tons per gigabytes, as in 30-year-old mainframe computers with vacuum tube circuits, to fractions of an ounce in today's miniaturized silicon microchip circuits. These are examples of dematerialization and miniaturization through design.

The building sector has had its share of visionaries preaching design through dematerialization, ephemeralization, and miniaturization. Among the most important was Buckminster Fuller, who, 60 years ago, was thinking about buildings as ecological systems. To some extent, intelligent design may reduce the initial input of materials in the building, but the key to dematerialization in buildings is likely to revolve around design for reuse and remanufacture. Modern materials—plastics, aluminum, steel, and composites—tend to have high-embodied energy. If they are deliberately designed for reuse and remanufacture, their initial metabolism and footprint is extended over many lives.

CONCLUSION

Over our history as a species, we have made fundamental leaps that expanded human consciousness, culture, and design—each time reshaping human experience, institutions, and environment in new directions. The long-term human cultural record and research into the behavior of dynamic complex systems supports the continuing possibility for fundamental changes in human consciousness. The changes I have in mind do not necessarily involve genetic evolution; they are more like new software to run our old hard-wired human selves.

In the 1950s, the cultural historian Jean Gebser described the era we are living in as "the late stage of mentally dominated consciousness; a world above the given world of nature." He and others have traced the 30,000-year history of human culture through distinct phases, from the magical world of our hunter–gatherer tribal forebears, through the development of complex agricultural societies grounded in myth, ritual, hierarchy and war, and moving into the current stage, which begins with the written word and mathematics. Symbols come to represent events in the real world, and the human mind and the culture it has created allows us to manipulate almost all elements in the living world.

Culture is expressed in what and how we build and use the land, water, and other resources. Today, the sights and the trends are not pretty. Satellite images reveal the blotchy, rapidly growing gray patches of mega-cities—sprawling, polluted prototypes of an urban future. The same dumb-design building templates are replicated globally. Good farmland and soils continue to be depleted at accelerating rates. Grasslands turn into deserts; forests into wastelands; rivers and coastal waters into stinking cesspools. Species are disappearing at a rate unparalleled since the catastrophic collision of meteors and Earth ended the age of the dinosaurs 60 million years ago. And everywhere on Earth, complex human communities and natural ecologies are destroyed and processed into economic commodities.

Our evolution as a species is not complete. The design of the human brain suggests that we are capable of greater good and greater wisdom if we can evolve the collective cultural forms that encourage all of us to realize our full potential as humans and as part of the larger flow of life. That is my hope—to build in a way that expresses that hope. And continuity can be our purpose. The barriers exist primarily in the flawed mechanistic mental models that still dominate political and corporate organization; and in the dangerous hegemony—still largely unchallenged—of conventional economics and its fatally flawed accounting system that fails to account for the "natural capital" of ecosystem services that cannot be replaced by any technological fix.

Biosphere II is also a cautionary tale for designers. We cannot recreate four billion years of evolution. But we can work to slow the rate at which things get worse; we can create environments in which people feel their connection to the pulse of nature's nurturing life forces, and in so doing help bring into being a consciousness and human nature that reveals to us the truth of our collective past and present, guiding us into a new ecologic future.

Presentation in Dialogue with Christopher Alexander, Esalen Institute, Big Sur, CA, 1991

The Pattern Language articulates in a systematic way a network of relationships that breathes life into design for people and nature. There is a lot of congruity between Chris's approach and my own ecological perspective. One of my mentors, who is both a very fine naturalist and a Jungian psychiatrist, looks at what we're doing in our modern world and chuckles, "It's like burning up the house of life in order to toast marshmallows." My passion is about the House of Life and how it relates to the marshmallow. There's a great congruence between the picture Chris paints on how we should design the man-made environment and how the natural world works because both work around his concept of Centers of Life. In our evolution as humans, we instinctively always moved to nature's center of life—where two systems meet, such as grassland and forest, the places of greatest diversity and productivity which ecology calls "Ecotones." Our human origin in Africa where savannah met forest was no accident.

I tend to experience multiple perspectives. When I experience cities and places with a high level of complexity, I experience both the productivity and its entropy. The difference between a living system such as a blue-green algae and Los Angeles is that the algae is coherent in the energetic sense, producing and holding on to energy, while Los Angeles simply consumes, perhaps transforming the energy into forms of consciousness and information. Perhaps the marriage of energetics and information is what life is about. We want to create "sustainable environments" which assumes we cannot have life for very long if we continue to degrade the Centers of Life in nature and design which support us. The conversation we had yesterday envisioned weaving the two—nature and design—together.

The means to weave the two types of Centers of Life together may require a further evolution in our consciousness, or perhaps a return to an earlier consciousness when humans had a much closer connection to the natural world. It's great that Chris's theory is present here at Esalen, because Esalen's agenda and purpose has been nurturing a new consciousness. I'm an optimist about possibilities and a pessimist about probabilities. I don't believe we can rush human evolution, or return it to some past state. Over the last few years, I've been trying to learn what the evolution of consciousness is all about and how it works. We know our human design has not changed since our human origin, but evidently our consciousness has. I agree with Chris that the kind of environment you are in can in itself trigger a shift in awareness. A critical number of shifts in awareness may produce a shift in consciousness. The environment is a powerful teacher, we both agree on that.

A lot of the energy behind places like Esalen, and other projects started in the 1960s, was that we believed that we could create or design a transformation in consciousness and accomplish that in ten or twenty years. Of course we were wrong. Design can play an important role in bringing about cultural change, and I do see a powerful congruence between Chris's concept of Centers of Life and its integration with ecological design.

There are three other concepts relating to ecology and design I'd like to discuss briefly. We've all heard "Sustainability," most of us are familiar with "conservation," and Bob Rodale often used the term "regeneration." "Conservation" is a "fund" concept. A good conservationist says we have to conserve our natural resources. The concern is the rate at which we spend what we have. Sustainability is a "flow" concept. We have a fixed stock of resources at any point in time, we spend them at some rate, and we reinvest to maintain the stock through recycling, replanting, or redesign for longer life. "Sustainable design" implies that our job is not only to design human habitation but to design the reinvestment, enhancement, and maintenance of natural systems. By this standard, anything remotely resembling how we in the most developed countries live is not sustainable because the outflow overwhelms any attempt to maintain stable flows of what nature provides. The concept of "regeneration" implies regrowth and healing. Rodale sees regeneration in conflict with traditional economic models that measure a society's well-being in dollar terms. The greater the GDP, or total financial transactions, the better off the society. Rodale's idea was if you had a healthy community, you had fewer economic transactions. If you had a vegetable garden and grew your own food and gave away your surplus, there was a negligible economic transaction. If the old lady next door was sick and needed a helping hand an hour a day, in a healthy community you'd take care of her and there was no money exchanged. Regeneration implies concern and care for the common good, both human and natural. It's the term that speaks most powerfully to me.

Further Reading: The Seminal Books of the Nineties

After the Clockwork Universe: The Emerging Science and Culture of Integral Society
by Sally J. Goerner, 1999

The Great Work: Our Way into the Future
by Thomas Berry, 1999

Biomimicry: Innovation Inspired by Nature
by Janine M. Benyus, 1997

When Corporations Rule the World
by David C. Korten, 1995

Awakening Earth: Exploring the Evolution of Human Culture and Consciousness
by Duane Elgin, 1993

The Ecology of Commerce: A Declaration of Sustainability
by Paul Hawken, 1993

The Eighties: The Lost Decade

The 1980 election of Ronald Reagan to President stopped the heady momentum of the environmental and design movements in their tracks. Reagan claimed, "It's morning again in America." Soon, it was reported in the news that "workmen have now taken down the solar water-heating system installed on the White House roof in 1979." Also in 1979, SERI, the Solar Energy Research Institute initiated by President Carter and headed by Denis Hayes, gave $250,000 to the Marin Solar Village Corporation to assist Van der Ryn and Calthorpe in developing a plan for a Solar Village on the site of Hamilton Air Force Base, on the major corridor north of San Francisco. Under the Surplus Property Act, the Federal government had offered this 1,100-acre waterfront plot to Marin County for $1.

We developed the plan, the first "sustainable community" in this country, integrating passive solar energy efficiency and on-site renewable energy with mass transit, on-site employment, wetlands restoration, and on-site food production, among many other features. Within months of taking office, the Reagan administration revoked the Surplus Property Act transfer and put the land up for sale to the highest bidder. I was devastated. Not long after, a large Peace Corps contract to train corps members in appropriate technology practices at our Farallones Institute was cancelled by the Reagan administration, putting the future of our Rural Center in jeopardy.

I then turned my attention to my home in the country, to writing a book with Peter Calthorpe, *Sustainable Communities*, to my teaching and writing, and to my life-long practice of watercolor painting in nature. Whenever I start a new building-design project, I begin with a day of sitting on site and painting, letting the site speak to me through my eyes, hands, brush, and the fluid watercolors. For 50 years I have painted watercolor landscapes, all over the world. It is a form of meditation, a way to get quiet and become aware of the subtleties of place—how light changes colors; the forms and patterns; the sounds and spaces. Watercolor painting helps me to actually feel and see fully, not just with the eyes and brain, but with my whole being. It's the difference between merely *looking,* which is passive involvement in place, and *seeing,* which is active involvement.

Without asking for it, I was handed a great gift that I was able to share with many students, beginning in the late 1980s and continuing for many years: Gary Brown, the gentle Chairman of the Architecture Department, had visited our office in Sausalito and had seen some of my watercolors hanging on the walls. "We haven't taught watercolor in the Department since the Beaux Arts days," he said. "Why don't you offer a class, Sim?" And so the next semester we offered Water Color Sketching Outdoors, which we described this way: "Watercolor sketching in the field is an unsurpassed and indispensible tool for all designers. Using a minimum of time and equipment, you learn to see, analyze, and record the feeling, character, color, and light of a place. Class sessions take place in a variety of Bay Area settings chosen for their unique natural and urban landscape features."

The course was scheduled for every Friday, leaving Berkeley at 9 a.m. and returning at 4 p.m. A van took the 12 to 15 students to many of my favorite places in the Bay Area, including a cemetery in Oakland, the San Francisco and Sausalito waterfronts, Sacramento Valley river towns, Napa Valley, and the Point Reyes Peninsula. I would spend 15 minutes doing a brief demonstration, emphasizing not to focus on objects but to look for edges of light, form, and color change. After that, everyone would find their spots, and the only rule was silence. No talking to one another or asking me questions. At 3:30, we would gather to look at the work, before taking the bus ride back to campus. Over the years, I've gotten feedback from former students who claim the class was a life-changing experience. When removed from the busy bustle of campus and classes, they reconnected with their inner selves and the living world of nature.

In today's university architecture studios, such primitive technologies as drawing and painting have been replaced with computers, which, with deft student fingers, tend to yield an empty colorful stream of architectural fantasies. And it's not just a problem with American architecture education. Patrik Schumacher, writing in the British *Architectural Review*, says he sees no future for the type of hopelessly unrealistic education lauded by the British architectural establishment. The submissions to the current RIBA President's Medals demonstrate once more that architectural education in Britain is operating in a parallel universe. The (best?) students of the current generation as well as their teachers seem to think that the ordinary life processes of contemporary society are too boring to merit the avant-garde's attention. Instead, we witness the invention of scenarios that are supposedly more interesting than the challenges actually posed by contemporary reality. The points of departure for the majority of projects are improbable narratives with intended symbolic message or poetic import … The result might be a provocation at best, but often ends up as nothing but naive (if not pompous) posturing. Success in the world is not to be expected from such pursuits.

"Integral Design," Sausalito, CA, 1988

We are ready for a new paradigm. In my 25 years in architecture, I have never seen it so intellectually bankrupt. The whole architectural profession seems to have given up its morale and its visionary role in society. And yet we are at a time when what we know and what we can do, as architects, is more important than ever before.

The real task seems to be to translate the rhetoric of the architect as the builder, the integrator, and the coordinator, into action. Having spent four years as State Architect in California, I can say that it is possible to do this. It's possible to talk sense to legislators and get them to do some very good things.

The real opportunity we have is the one that results from designing with limited resources and beginning to become aware of the opportunities that grow out of the depletable nature of our resources. What this means to me is what I am going to define as "integral design," in which architecture becomes not only building but an orchestration of the other forms of energy that are designed into the form of the built environment. We need to consider what happens to the waste generated by buildings, as well as the energy that is involved in creating a building and the energy that is involved in maintaining it.

The decisions that we make will be paid for by people many years down the road. Our children don't inherit the world from us; we are simply borrowing it from them. The decisions I make in my work are going to influence those after me, just as the ones you make are going to affect future generations.

We need to look in a more integrative way at how we orchestrate everything that makes up a life-support system—not just shelter and the habitable environment, but food, energy, waste, and all the things that are part of the system. The kind of paradigm we need to develop is one in which we begin to look more closely at what happens in the natural world. When I went to architecture school—and I suspect it hasn't changed that much in 25 years—I went through six years of training and never took a course in natural science. In architectural curricula, you study dead things such as concrete; there is no study of botany or even geology. This missing ingredient was bypassed in the great revolution that took place in architectural education in the 1920s, although the people in the Bauhaus movement were aware of forces that constitute the missing ingredient. They were never integrated into how we think and how we design, and that is the major focus of what I am working on now. So if it seems my ideas relate more to agriculture or biology, it's on purpose. We need to look much more closely at how natural systems work, and we must learn from them.

Integral design is about creating living places or habitats, the humanly created organization of which is analogous to the features of a healthy natural system. By doing this, we can begin to approximate the economy, the efficiency, and the simple elegance that is inherent in any natural system. The work we use to describe the tendency to approximate the features of a natural system is "integral"—connected or unified. The dictionary meaning of integral is "essential to completeness."

It's important to keep in mind that no humanly designed system can ever achieve the organization that natural systems have evolved over millions of years. But we must keep in mind that integral design has as much to do with process as it does with realized form. A house whose shape is analogous to a nautilus shell, or a dome emulating the microscopic structure of an organism, is not inherently organic. Process must be analogous as well as shape, although we do tend to think of houses built with natural materials, like earth, stone or unsawn wood, as more natural than those built with industrial materials such as glass, steel, or concrete. Integral design applies the lessons of the biology and ecology of the natural systems to the design of environments for people. This emerging kind of integration of architecture and biology, dubbed "bio-tecture" or "eco-tecture," is in its infancy, although we can already begin to identify principles and patterns.

An obvious question is, "Why emulate natural design?" What is there about the behavior of natural systems that we should pay attention to in designing our cities, towns, and houses? The answer is framed by the most natural observed event on Earth. The source of all light energy is the sun, but the Earth is only habitable through the action of green plants, from lowly algae to towering redwoods, which capture only about 1 percent of solar energy and transform it into useful forms of energy for all life. Without these complex natural systems to fix and transform energy, all solar energy would be lost as waste heat and life could not be sustained.

We express this process as entropy: the tendency of all energy to degrade into unusable waste heat radiated back into space. The opposite is negentropy, which is the sum total of all life processes that capture and transform energy into usable form. It is negentropy, the work of all the silent plants and bacteria, the entire complex of natural systems, which is the basis for life and civilization, the savings that we accrue through natural systems.

Evolution is a process by which natural systems become increasingly diverse, complex, and differentiated, in order to counteract entropy. Evolution, through negentropy, may be seen as nature's slow but certain strategy to achieve stability in the face of the inevitable degradation and eventual death of the planet.

Human beings cannot hope to improve on the efficiency of natural negentropic processes, but we should be able to design habitats and culture in such a way that natural systems, and the information in them, are not degraded. If natural systems are degraded, then human cultural evolution will be degraded and destroyed.

Humans, as a species, are uniquely adapted to storing information in abstract and symbolic forms, and this gives us our unique ability to manipulate our surroundings as no other species can. It's interesting that some people claim that modern societies are more callous about their effect on natural systems than were earlier peoples. In truth, while there are important exceptions, the rule seems to be that most cultures have been callous about their natural systems and environments. Throughout history, cultures have gained short-term advantage by juggling what ecologists call "early succession-type" monocultures, and as ecosystems deteriorated through early succession-type monocultures, people had to take the consequences and move on. In Edward Hyams's book *Soil and Civilization*, he documents the ecological destruction of vast areas of the planet by earlier cultures. We don't have to suffer heavy guilt about modern industrial society as destroyer: most cultures have destroyed their environments. So we don't have a corner on ignorance (although we do seem to be in the lead).

Hyams points out that most of the cultures he talks about were destroyed by the use of early succession monoculture techniques, characterized by the production of large yields for relatively short periods of time. It's like the story of the goose that laid the golden egg. The keepers, not satisfied with getting the eggs one at a time, killed the goose to get them all at once—only to find that once the goose was dead there were no more golden eggs to be had. That old parable is very relevant today.

What has changed from earlier cultures is our increased potential for the destruction of natural systems, provided by a dizzying array of new technology and the increasing insulation of modern urban populations from the effects of ecological deterioration. We have a false sense of security provided by a massive but short-lived supply of fossil fuels—oil and gas, which are simply the stored products of negentropic systems many eons old.

We can do something about this situation by learning how to make the transition to an integrally designed way of life.

It all requires much time to give a definitive picture of what distinguishes a living system from an inanimate one, or how to construct a habitat that fully integrates the inanimate and the living form. At this time, only the vague outline is there, and much of what is learnable must be learned by comparison. We can contrast the properties of the integral system with what I call the linear system—the characteristic early-succession ecology in monocultures that has dominated most human societies. What may look to you like a very complex society, in ecological terms may actually be in a very simple and early-succession stage. In the integral system, energy flows through loops; in linear systems, energy flows in straight lines. In integral systems, parts fit overlapping functions; in the linear system, parts are specialized components. Integral systems have low entropy and high information. In the integral system, memory is stored in many different cells. In the linear system, memory is stored in specialized components—such as architects. In integral systems, there is a high rate of material recovery; in a linear system, there is a high rate of material loss. Integral systems have multiple alternate channels; linear systems have single channels. Integral systems have no waste; linear systems have high waste. These properties exist on a continuum, and we need to develop a feeling for when a particular system approaches the integral or linear.

There are four processes unique to integral systems:

1. They process materials and energy through closed loops and webs of multiple channels. The closed loop is absolutely fundamental to the nature of living systems, and many benefits are realized from the intentional application of this concept to the built environment. Living organisms exist as complex eddy pools in a continuously flowing stream of energy and material elements. That energy from the sun, which is caught by life processes, is sooner or later radiated away into space, where it is forever lost to us. It takes many millions of years for nutrient elements to be recycled back into the land, and the trickle of energy and nutrients available is not infinite and must be conserved. They are conserved in natural systems through closed loops and the webbing of closed loops. That is what food chains are all about—attempts to capture that radiant energy from the sun and prevent it from being lost as waste heat. The loops of natural systems allow both cycling and self-regulation. Each sub-system regulates its input to release outputs, which can inhibit the process that made them.

2. They release energy in the system in small increments, contributing to homeostasis, the stability in natural systems. Energy is most efficiently

used by organisms in small increments. Mature natural systems consist of many different stages, each of which can store energy for a long time and transport it along a multiplicity of routes and channels. This has the effect of minimizing waste, since, when a sudden surge of potential energy is released in a simple system, very little of it can be stored.

3. They maintain a steady state, or homeostasis, through negative feedback and permeable boundaries. The web of electrical distribution is designed as a multiple channel so that power companies can shuttle excess power from one place to another. But we still have black-outs in New York and other places. The electrical webs are not quite multiple enough to prevent complete breakdowns. In an integral system, boundaries are permeable and systems mesh together with such intricacy that transactions across the boundaries of systems flow, without waste or upheaval. By contrast, our modern urban systems are monocultural crazy quilts, stitched loosely together with waste. We all know what happens when potential energy is released in a simple system and very little of it can be stored, such as when a watershed is denuded of vegetation and can no longer absorb a heavy rain. Downstream flooding results, with a loss of soil and water and a further regression of the natural system. In an ecosystem, many little steps tend to be gentle and subtle, while a few big steps tend to be harsh and destructive.

4. They store information in a decentralized genetic memory. Information is the pattern that organizes form. The energy–materials pattern is form; and the pattern, when transmitted, is information. In simplest terms, "inform" means to give form to. Within any living system, evolutionary information is contained in the DNA of every cell and in the learned experience of the food chain. DNA is the code that determines the form and organization of the organism. In human societies, information is stored in cultural patterns, including the built environment, institutional structures, and the patterns of communication. It is very important to look at this relationship between information and form, which starts with energy flow. The pattern of energy flow is, in fact, information and culture.

In the continuing cycle of energy and materials through time, information is stored as genetic evolution in culture. Information is precious and needs to be conserved. While species have continuously appeared and disappeared throughout Earth history, every major information advance has been retained. The real harvest of the ecological fabric evolving through time is information, including human culture. Returning to a higher degree of regional autonomy or individual responsibility will not be a return to the Dark Ages, as some have claimed, as long as information is conserved and enhanced. It is a necessary accommodation to the ecological rules by which living beings can maintain themselves in a healthy relationship with their world.

Those points may sound like the jargon of electronics and circuitry, and indeed it is. The language we use to explain the flow of energy and materials in natural systems has been adapted to humanly designed systems. However, the ecological reality is more complex, less mechanistic, and more indeterminate than any reality man is capable of constructing.

Marshall McLuhan was one of the first people to look at our culture in terms of conserved and enhanced information. We think there is a lot of information in our culture, don't we? We pick up a copy of *T.V. Guide* and think, "Boy, there's a lot of information in there!" Not so. The extent to which we standardize and go for massive solutions is the extent to which we destroy information. Consider the debate about the snail darter stopping the $120 million Tennessee Valley Authority (TVA) dam. Now that is a parable about information. That snail darter, as a species in a genetic evolutionary chain, contains more information than that damn dam does!

An overload, a surge of energy flowing through a system, can be destructive to its information content. That is a paradigm of modern culture. We have an overload of energy flowing through this system and it is destructive information—it doesn't enhance it. This applies to natural as well as to man-made systems. Run too much current through an appliance and it burns itself out. Overload an aquatic system with nutrients suspended in sewage and its natural health and structure is destroyed. Monocultures process energy and materials so rapidly that the outflow overwhelms systems on the receiving end, and the result is a loss of information and structure.

Economists, those shaman of the modern industrial system, unfortunately know nothing about the behavior of natural systems. In economics, flow is everything, as measured in money. The destruction of information embedded in the structure of living communities is not measured, and the increased entropy that results from the loss of information is never calculated. Keynesian economics seeks to maximize energy and money flow, while stable and diverse natural and cultural systems are seen as obstacles to progress, as resources to be transformed into cash flow. I see this as burning down the house of life in order to toast marshmallows. This relationship also explains the paradox of inflation without growth. We are developing a system with more and more entropy, but with a greater and greater GNP. There is more flow of money transactions, but no real increase in the quality of life as measured in the structure of information.

The distribution of information in living systems varies with their scale and function, but an analogy can be drawn between the three basic life scales—ecosystems, organisms, and cells—and the concept of information can be related to each of these three levels of life.

An ecosystem has five characteristics: it fixes sunlight into a biomass; it cycles nutrients; it is self-regulating in population size; its species succeed each other; and it is self-producing and self-maintaining. The structure of information in the ecosystem follows the general principles that I have already discussed: the presence of negative feedback loops; the existence of boundaries between distinct sub-systems; and information centralized in each cell. An ecosystem can last indefinitely and compensate for major disturbances and dislocations. A lost part or species can usually be compensated for by other parts with a similar function. Information is retained within the genetic, and sometimes learned, patterns of other species.

Man cannot design an ecosystem, and no humanly designed system ever has all of those characteristics of an ecosystem. Gardens and some agricultural systems are comparable to natural systems, and one can design a habitat and whole system—including food and waste—that is built in paths, steps, and loops, like an ecosystem. Buildings designed this way will have more stable and healthy systems, but these systems will also be less adaptive to producing the characteristic monocultural surge of quick rise-and-fall cultures.

Organisms are much more centralized with regard to information, especially animals with central nervous systems. They have comparatively little redundancy of functioning parts. We have two kidneys, but only one brain, and the loss of an important organ commonly results in death, although the highly directed and organized parts allow the organism to focus energy very effectively while alive. The organ is the real analogue of the machine; when people understood how organisms

Santa Fe Storm Sunset

worked even at a very elemental level, they were in a position to design machines.

Houses are like bodies, in that their components are designed, like organs, to accomplish specific functions, and you can build in some degree of back-up to compensate for changes and breakdowns. In the house-as-organism, the information is centralized in the humans who operate the household systems. This is another thing that designers tend to forget, and I've had colossal battles with the bureaucracy over this point. I like to think of a window or wall as a dynamic object that people can change, but bureaucrats don't like that. They think that, unless a window is triple-glazed, it's just losing heat. Suppose you put an insulated drape in front of it? Yes, they say, but we can't depend on people to close the drape when it is cold. Do you see where that attitude takes us? The fact that bureaucrats feel they have to protect us from our own stupidity brings us up to a lot of problems. The user has become an anonymous participant, or a non-participant, in the objects and environment designed for him or her.

A cell is the intermediary between ecosystem and organism and design. Its information is relatively centralized in its nucleus, but it has many parallel and redundant metabolism channels, so the cell combines the potential for immortality with the direction of energy toward a specific task. Communities resemble cell tissues in their spatial arrangement and metabolic looping. If you look at slides of cell tissues, they look amazingly like cities from an aerial view. That is not a coincidence. To the extent that communities, or cells, conserve energy or materials effectively, they place less strain on the surrounding and supporting systems.

Farallones Institute is a group of designers, scientists, and engineers that I founded about six years ago to begin to put some of these ideas into practice. One of the first things we did was to take an old house in Berkeley and redesign it along some of these principles I am discussing. The Integral Urban House was designed so that each major functional system employs multiple pathways from material and energy flow. The heating system, for example, includes direct solar gain through windows; a solar air space heating system; and a wood stove space heater for cloudy, cold days. Organic waste can be shunted in a variety of ways. Human fecal matter decomposes in a composting toilet and, when fully decomposed, is used as a soil amendment on ornamental plants. Urine is collected and used as a nitrogen-rich fertilizer. Kitchen scraps are fed to the chickens and converted into edible protein, and the chicken manure is recycled in the garden. Garbage can also be composted or fed into worm cultures to make a nutrient-rich casting for garden use, and the worms can then be fed to the chickens or to the fish in the pond. Duckweed in the pond absorbs toxic fish waste, and in turn can be dried and fed to the chickens. These are all multiple loops. The house is there; all these loops are operating. It's amazing to see the light go on in people as they see these abstractions become real and as they figure out how to apply an idea to their own homes.

The principle of multiple pathways is closely linked to the idea of diversity and stability of healthy, natural systems, and the multiple pathway is an interactive process within any food or nutrient chain. For example, in a healthy garden, you want to have a diversity of plants, which insures that there is going to be a diversity of insect life associated with those plants. That creates a situation where no particular insect population is likely to get out of control and become a pest. Agriculture is slowly beginning to realize this principle of diversity in crops. The use of pesticides is a positive feedback cycle: devote one area, the Midwest for example, to one crop such as corn, and that generates a predator that gets totally out of control. You use pesticides, but the insects become more resistant and you have to apply more and more pesticide. That's a positive feedback cycle.

This idea of integral loops enhancing stability and diversity can be contrasted with its linear equivalent. To heat a house electrically requires the consumption of more times the amount of energy in high-quality fuels than will finally result in useful heat in the home. The methods we use to heat our homes with electricity are like using a nuclear powered chainsaw to cut butter. The linear mode we use to dispose of what we call "wastes" simply hauls waste to landfills, and most urban areas are now running out of available landfill areas, not surprisingly. Cities are forced to haul garbage to remote locations hundreds of miles away. Human waste is diluted to a ratio of 100 to 1 with potable water, and then piped to large sewage factories, where the solids are removed with mechanical and bacterial action. The polluted, nutrient-rich effluent that remains is dumped into the river or ocean, where it overloads the ability of natural systems to provide oxygen. This produces a condition known as eutrophication, in which there is a surge of microbiological and algae growth, which then depletes the oxygen and fouls up the water.

Another feature of the multiple pathway is that each component of this system tends to perform overlapping functions, and one test of the integral quality of any system is the extent to which components are integrated into multiple functions. An electric heater can only be an electric heater. A garbage truck can only be a garbage truck. However, a window admits light, provides a view, and can also be a solar-energy collector. A greenhouse attached to a window can be a solar collector and a storage system, or a place to grow seedlings and winter vegetables, or even the location for a hot tub, which we Californians are fond of. A planting box, however small, together with composting buckets, takes the place of the smelly garbage and the noisy garbage truck. Besides processing waste nutrients, it provides a source of food and flowers, and can be the focus for many pleasant leisure hours.

In terms of human purpose, integral design produces value in three spheres: economy, energy use, and esthetics. Economics measures the short-term cost of energy and material transactions in money terms. Costs are set by the availability of and demand for materials and services, as well as by other constraints of the marketplace, such as government actions, which affect or distort the economic transactions. The individual decision maker is concerned with costs that his or her actions can directly affect … and a production-oriented economy based on low-priced fossil fuels and so on. That integral design, in itself, very often does not result in short-term economic advantages for its practitioner is a very important fact. Chances are that if you go out and attempt any of the wonderful things I'm advising now, it may not compete in the marketplace in economic terms. In the short run, a farmer who grows diversified crops and returns waste to the soil may not do as well as the farmer whose profits are gained at the expense of strip mining the soil of its nutrients and quality. The urban dweller who expends the effort to install a waterless recycling toilet still has to pay the tax burden of a wasteful centralized sewage system. The homeowner who installs solar heating equipment still has to underwrite the cost of expensive, conventional, centralized generating equipment and must compete against the relatively low price of fossil fuels. In each case, the boundaries of the economic system do not mesh with the boundaries of the natural or integral system. The costs of destroying the fertility of the soil are not charged against the soil miner, and there are no economic incentives offered to the individual who does not wish to participate in institutionalized pollution such as that which is practiced in the public sewer.

However, as our way of life runs up against the limits imposed by resource scarcity, the breakdowns

in its overextended networks, and the simple entropy of its bloated size, economics will begin to reflect the advantages of working with the natural grain, rather than against it. The balance is changing, and a future generation of designers that blindly repeats the mistakes of previous generations, those that grew up without energy as a consideration, will be out of business. If you treat natural systems as a view to be looked at through a Thermopane window, there won't be any work for you. Work in the future will be in terms of restoring the balance.

In any integrally designed system, total energy flow will be lower than in a linear system, where energy pulses through to achieve maximum product flow and a high rate of waste. The economic costs are not borne by the immediate user, but get buried in the increasing entropy of larger systems. Nuclear electricity is a good example: the costs are buried in the entire rate base, so you don't know what you are paying for. And a very important point to keep in mind is that a high flow-through does not necessarily imply a high product. Modern agriculture uses 10 to 60 calories of energy to produce one calorie of food; it uses more energy to produce than it turns out. In traditional agriculture, that ratio is reversed. In China, it takes one calorie of energy—mostly human—to produce 30 calories of food. But there's more to the equation. You also have to look at how much comes out the end of the pipeline. Our agricultural practices are rationalized on the basis that the total productivity of energy-intensive agriculture is higher than traditional methods, and that we would starve without energy-intensive agriculture. Food prices would be astronomical if the current fossil-fuel subsidy of agriculture was removed. At a time when our food system is so dependent on energy-wasteful monocultures, that claim is all too sadly true. But more than anything else, it points out the need to rebuild the network of regional energy systems in agriculture before it is too late.

The concept of flow is a very important one. It's not just the ratio of energy used; it's also the concept of the total flow. Integral design tends to reduce the energy flow and use and integrate more fully into smaller, more decentralized units. For example, we have begun to design food production back into neighborhoods and the home by way of garden vegetables. Even this, as limited as it may be, is very important because it is an energy multiplier.

Esthetics are too often neglected, but without them neither economy nor efficiency of energy would have meaning. Indeed, esthetics is the meaning that we find in form. As conceptual information, it varies from culture to culture. The meaning we derive from the environment is limited both by the form of that environment and how we are able to interact with it. A friend of mine from an industrial area of the Midwest commented that, while he and his neighbors were surrounded by ecological devastation they were "tool-literate," because they were surrounded by a forest of tools and machines. Our active participation and interaction with complex and diverse living systems increases our awareness and renews the spirit. In short, the meaning that we derive from life is enriched and constantly recharged by our functional and ritualistic connections to the natural world. If you examine the pre-industrial esthetic, you'll see that it was always based on that kind of connection, whether it takes the form of a miniature Japanese garden, a simple Arab courtyard fountain, or the shade elms of a New England commons. It constituted a whole picturesque "architecture without architects" of an earlier world that adapted habitat to local materials, site, climate, and ecosystem. The important thing about esthetics is not how something looks, but the kind of participation it brings about with the natural system. That is where the esthetic has to be derived from, not from the empty banterings of the architectural establishment.

For the most part, Americans have lost that

"INTEGRAL DESIGN," SAUSALITO, CA, 1988

intimate connection and awareness of their place in the natural world. The "natural" has been reduced to empty symbols, such as the tract-house lawn, which originally started as a sheep meadow (the lawn was there because the sheep cropped the grass—but now the sheep have been replaced by lawn mowers). Ecosystems have become dim landscapes to be appreciated out of a car window, another low-information object like the TV screen.

The task, then, of integral design, is to begin to recreate the opportunities for people to derive meaning and satisfaction from their experience with natural cycles. This assumes that people become active and intelligent participants in managing and maintaining their environment. The hot rod is an example of an esthetic that grew out of our attempt to find meaning in everyday industrial culture. Maybe the day is not too far off when millions of Americans will be hot-rodding their now denatured houses into finely tuned, multi-channel, closed-loop, organic instruments for processing nature's flow.

"The Next Urban Transformation," Sausalito, CA, 1985

In the ten-thousand-year history of cities, there have only been two significant transitions which have shaped urban form: the transition to agriculture, and the transition to machine age. A third transition is coming, brought about by the declining availability of cheap fossil-fuel energy. In the past century, it has been cheap energy which has permitted cities to expand logarithmically by using low-cost, high-quality energy to support every aspect of urban life. If the city is to survive, it will have to be designed for sustainability, balancing its resource use with continuously available supplies.

The first cities were made possible by the invention of agriculture and written forms of communication. The domestication of plants made it possible to grow food at fixed times and at fixed locations, and the storage of harvests made it possible to sustain the non-agricultural urban dweller. Written communication supported societal structure larger than the village. The size, shape, and location of cities up until the Industrial Revolution were largely limited by the need to maintain a local supply of food, water, and fuel, and until modern times there were few cities with more than a hundred thousand people.

The second great urban transformation began with the invention of machines powered with fossil fuels and the proliferation of a science and technology that could disassemble nature into its parts on a large scale, and also synthesize organic materials from non-living matter. Many of these urbanizing technologies are chronicled by the historian Siegfried Giedion in his classic work, *Mechanization Takes Command*. Giedion points out that the growth of the great American urban centers, which expanded rapidly after the Civil War, was directly connected to the invention of the mechanical reaper, the flour milling machine, the assembly line slaughter of hogs, the railroad, the steamship, and Pasteur's discovery of heat sterilization to destroy bacteria and preserve food.

Mechanized food production, mechanized food processing, improved food storage, and rail transportation freed cities to expand in size beyond the constraints of their local and seasonal food base. During the late nineteenth and early twentieth centuries, cities also developed the rudiments of other key services necessary for urban growth, such as central water supply, and indoor plumbing to supply potable water and carry away wastes.

With the basic needs for food, water, and sanitation resolved, the stage was set for the city to uncouple entirely from the limitations of place, the local resource base, and the rhythms and cycles of nature. The late nineteenth and early twentieth centuries saw a propagation of technologies which completed the transition to the Industrial City: central heating using coal, natural gas, and oil;

the development of electric generation facilities and distribution systems; the electric light and electric motor; the internal combustion engine and automobile; the telephone; mechanical refrigeration and air conditioning; the high speed elevator; machine-made glass; fabricated metals.

And so, although there have been many changes, the essential fabric of modern urban life was created a few brief generations ago, within the lifetimes of our parents, grandparents, and their parents. It is all so familiar to us that it has become a part of us, and we, part of it.

The city as we know it does not make visible the processes that are responsible for sustaining life. The city becomes an invasion and an assault on alien territory. It ignores natural conditions and natural systems. Indeed, the main thing about the city is that it is hard, mechanical, straight-edged. What once was natural landscape is transformed. Vegetation is assigned to a park, occasional street ornamentation, or allowed in the form of weeds in a vacant lot. Natural watercourses are erased and storm water channeled into underground pipes or streams that become concrete-lined ditches. The soil is covered with concrete. Hills and other natural features are graded into building sites. Wetlands are drained and filled. The boundaries denoting different ownerships and uses do not respect natural boundaries but follow the Descartian logic of the surveyor. The celestial rhythm of sun, moon, and stars is obscured by electric light at night and polluted air by day. Time is marked by the clock. Climate is altered by building patterns and the burning of hydrocarbons in cars and buildings. The diversity of creatures with whom we share the planet is reduced in the city to a few domesticated mammals and the hearty species who have adapted to urban life: rats, pigeons, cockroaches, and the like.

In the city, water flows from the tap although the source may have been a mountain stream a thousand miles distant. Body wastes are floated away down a ceramic receptacle to an unknown destination. Garbage is ground up in the sink and other detritus dumped into a chute or can from which it disappears. Food that has been assembled from points all over the globe is purchased in stores. Buildings are cool when it is warm outside, and warm inside when it is cold out. Forty percent of the land area of many cities is given over to the automobile and eight-lane freeways are clogged with people going from home to work and back again. Fuel for automobiles is dispensed at strategic locations from underground tanks. Electricity for lighting, heating, and electrically operated tools and appliances is instantly available at 12-foot intervals along the walls of every inhabited room. This is our everyday reality, how the world works, or at least how it has worked up to now.

These extraordinary events are the everyday stuff of urban existence, and many people's understanding of how the world works is limited to the physical reality I have described. The information and experience of the city dweller is bound up to the Mechanical/Industrial paradigm. And, even the well-informed urban resident tends to be ignorant of the underlying context and patterns which make it all possible. Instead of gazing at the stars on a moonless night, they go to the movie theater to see *Star Wars*.

In teaching about urban self-reliance over the years, it's always amazing to discover the fundamental lack of awareness of so many urban dwellers. At a ten-week course in Whole Systems at the Farallones Rural Center in Northern California, one student, a successful professional designer from an Eastern city, refused to eat fresh vegetables grown in the garden because they didn't look the same as the ones she was used to in the store. Another student disappeared each day to use the flush toilet at the local gas station because she could not bring herself to use the waterless, composting toilet. Most people have a very sketchy idea, if any at all, of where their water, electricity, or food come from or what happens to their wastes. What passes for functional knowledge in a big city may be dysfunctional elsewhere in space and time.

I believe we are entering a third great transformation in urban life which over the next 50 years will be as far-reaching and fundamental as the other two great transformations I have briefly outlined. The success of the Industrial City has been based on two conditions. First, the ability to convert one-time stocks of high-quality, fossil-fuel energy into useful forms of energy and work; and second, the ability to extract raw materials from a global hinterland in order to keep cities supplied. These conditions are rapidly changing. We are using up the easily accessible fossil fuels at a rapid rate and within several generations the cost of remaining fuels will be so great that their use will have to be reserved for essential non-substitutable uses. Industrial urban society depends on fossil fuels for every facet of life support and it is this energy that keeps city life flowing. It moves people and goods and keeps buildings habitable. In California, the biggest single user of electricity is the system that pumps water to the Los Angeles desert basin, and automobile use is the single biggest energy user, followed by the energy use in buildings. It takes an equivalent of six gallons of oil per day to maintain the average person in an urban lifestyle.

The use of the rest of the non-urbanized planet as a mine to supply cities also has a limited lifespan as natural systems are depleted and degraded. The planet is not inexhaustible, nor is nature, when abused, infinitely patient. That may also be said for the peoples who live in those areas whose resources support urban life. Without fossil fuels in continued abundance, urban life will have to be restructured into more sustainable patterns.

Sustainability implies some broad principles from an urban design point of view. First, sustainability implies that the use of energy and materials in an urban area be in balance with what the region can supply continuously through natural processes such as photosynthesis, biological decomposition, and the biogeochemical processes that support life. The immediate implications of this principle are a vastly reduced energy budget for cities and a smaller, more compact urban pattern interspersed with productive areas to collect energy, grow crops for food, fiber, and energy, and recycle wastes. New urban technologies will become less dependent on fossil fuels and rely more on a careful integration with biological processes. For example, organic wastes, including sewage and decomposable materials, can be recycled back into the soil, rather than, as is the rule today, dumped into oceans, burned, or used for landfills. Non-renewable materials and metals will be recycled. The design of urban support systems will be tied more intimately to the regional resource base rather than depending on global supply lines which are stretched to the limit. Cities will begin to rely on their regional ecosystems to produce most of the food and water consumed. This will mean cities of far greater design diversity than we have today, with each region developing unique urban forms based on regional characteristics that have long been overridden by cheap energy, which is a great leveler of regional diversity and the unique character of place.

A city that relies more on its own resources relies more on the skills and abilities of its own people. Today's urban dweller leads a split existence of eight hours as a "producer" in the workplace and the rest of the time as a "consumer" at home and elsewhere. In the sustainable city, these split roles will be reintegrated. The homeplace, rather than being merely the site of consumption, might through its very design produce some of its own food and energy as well as become a locus for work by its residents. The designs of the New Alchemy Ark in Woods Hole, Massachusetts, and the Farallones Institute Integral Urban House in Berkeley, California, are early experiments towards creating sustainable habitats that integrate food and energy production at the small scale.

However, urban self-reliance cannot be an individual affair. In a city, no one is a tight little island, and survival is a collective enterprise. Constructive action must be cooperative. The conditions that are pushing us to seek new ways of living in the city will, if we are creative, cooperative, and not paralyzed by fear, move us to new and richer experiences of community and the natural world.

How will the next urban transformation take place? What will it look like? The creation of sustainable cities and self-reliant communities, if it is to occur, starts with individual awareness and a change in personal values and perceptions; without this process, it is unlikely that cities can survive at all.

Some change will be forced by the new reality of limited fuel supplies. In another generation, the long solo auto commute will be a thing of the past. People will live closer to their work or ride the bus. The largest cities will break up into smaller, more manageable pieces. The continued growth of sophisticated telecommunications and computer technologies will make it possible for more kinds of work to be done in the home. The building stock will continue to be tuned up to conserve precious fuel, although many sealed-glass high-rise buildings will be abandoned or torn down and their materials reused because the energy to keep these buildings habitable will simply not be available. The average modern office building uses the equivalent of about a gallon of oil each year to heat, cool, and light every square foot of space, or the equivalent of a sizable oil well under each anachronistic commercial monument. Some of the asphalt areas that now cover our cities to park, service, and move autos will be torn up to grow food. The utility grid will become a two-way network with communities feeding locally generated power back into the grid to supplement today's remote fossil-fuel and nuclear power stations. People will spend less of their time working to satisfy their needs indirectly through wage labor, and more time maintaining their own lives directly through their own labor and that of their friends and neighbors.

I see the possibility for a city which is infinitely richer and more satisfying than what we know today. Whether in fact we can make this transition is the major challenge facing us today. Civilization as we know it, is an urban civilization, and the story of what happens to our cities will by and large be the story of what happens to our culture and civilization. I hope it's a story with a happy ending.

"Little America," *Le Monde*, 1981

The government released the preliminary 1980 census results for our area and it showed that the coastal communities lost population between 1970 and 1980. The story was cause for general amusement and satisfaction by the natives. Officially half of us don't exist, which is fine with us, although the tax man knows we're here so unfortunately we still get to pay our share of the new administration's fascination with defending us against starving Central American peasants and an aging Politburo in Moscow which seems to have its hands full keeping bread on Russia's table.

In a recent national poll, a majority of Americans said they preferred to live in small towns rather than big cities, and the census shows that in most parts of the country, small towns have indeed increased in size. Anyone who has lived here a while—I've been here ten years now—knows the census is wrong, and it is wrong for a particular reason. People don't want to be counted by Washington. People don't want to be statistics in someone else's game.

The small towns that stretch along the rugged Northern California coast from the Golden Gate Bridge north of San Francisco extending five hundred miles to Oregon are doing well. Point Reyes with less than a thousand people has its own weekly newspaper and for a while this year even had two. Last year, the *Point Reyes Light* owned and managed by two young journalists, Dave and Cathy Mitchell, won the coveted Pulitzer Prize for their reporting on Synanon. Synanon, founded by a gruff charismatic ex-alcoholic named Charles Dederich, started operating a rehabilitations center for drug addicts in Southern California in the late fifties and ten years later had established major centers in Northern California, including two in our area. Thanks to corporate giving, aggressive salesmanship, good press, and the support of most of the official establishment, Synanon became big business, and then as Dederich slipped back into alcohol and the premature senility that only absolute monarchy can produce, Synanon started pushing people around. Mitchell took them on (I thought him somewhat impetuous and foolhardy, a little like a déjà vu Citizen Kane), but he stuck to his guns, and got a much needed public focus on what was rapidly becoming a cult responsible only to its own absolutist leaders and goals. Rumor has it that *The Light* got the Pulitzer because the Pulitzer establishment wanted to show that small town papers are alive and well. They needn't have bothered because they are. And the publicity the Mitchells received cost them money, since afterward, they spent so much time flying around the country receiving congratulations from strangers.

There are two Americas. One is the "official America" reported and analyzed by media located in Washington, New York, and often Los Angeles. This is the America of government, big business, and the media itself. These three entities are like marble statues in a great hall of mirrors and what is seen is a multiple reflection of themselves and what is heard is an amplification of their own echo. Just as in the Industrial Age, surplus materials become pollution, clogging rivers, air, and land with wastes, so in the Information Age, information becomes pollution.

The other America, I call "Little America." This is the America outside the Hall of Mirrors. Little America lies in the shadow of the Great Hall but sees and hears the images, and the noise of the Hall from the perspective of its own terrain. Little America is rooted in and on a landscape of unique and familiar places. This America does not always share the images and tones of the Great Hall. One way that some inhabitants of Little America choose where they are is to shut out the stream of words and images that flow from the Great Hall. In my own case, this means no TV for the past 14 years and I find I'm less bored, less angry, and have seen more sunsets than before. I am more aware of where I am. TV seems to be a connection for those who don't feel connected.

The "official future" holds most Americans in its sway. They work for its corporations, live in its mass-produced environments, eat its franchised food, consume its advertised produccts. But dependence is not congruent with being belief. Polls show a declining faith in the promises and institutions of the official future. The Silent Majority of the Sixties that Richard Nixon identified as middle-class middle America fed up with liberalism has emerged as a vocal and well-disciplined Moral Majority tuned to TV priest preaching social Darwinism presided over by a corporate God who lives in a Heavenly country club.

But the Silent Majority of the Eighties inhabit Little America. They are the 75 percent of Americans who didn't vote for Ronald Reagan; they are the 52 percent that didn't vote at all in the national elections. They are the people who know that the Republicans and Democrats are like two sports teams owned by the same entrepreneur. We Little Americans see that relevant politics is the politics they can have a voice in and that is the politics close to home. Little Americans are decentralists sometimes separatists. Little Americans are watching the carefully cued play in Washington proclaiming a "mandate" to cut the budget while in fact what happens is the budget is *increased* over the previous administration by shifting money from social programs to an already swollen and bloated war budget. Little Americans are watching a desperate gamble whereby it is assumed that if we do our utmost, and believe strongly enough, we can rescue a system that has failed us. Ronald Reagan is indeed the smiling hero out of a 40-year-old movie, genially proclaiming a future which in the meantime has already come and gone.

Reagan understands the exterior of Little America and his rhetoric often plays to its concerns. But he is *President* hence the symbol of all that is obsolete and dangerous. And he is the willing leader and instrument of the very forces which threaten the health, uniqueness, and stability of our region of Little America. Our precious coast has become a resource mine for our now wealthiest neighbors on the Pacific Rim. The Japanese have already cleaned our forests and our fisheries and now in the hope that coastal waters may yield a few days of U.S. oil supply, the Secretary of the Interior James Watt has ordered the sale of offshore tracts to oil companies. More than any single act, this has made Little America, Northern California Region, *mad* as hell. Environmental groups, lulled into somnolence by success and the lip service of politicians, are adding new members by the thousands. People are genuinely startled to see an authentic nineteenth-century museum curiosity in the form of our Secretary of the Interior, a man to whom nature exists to serve man and nothing else. James Watt is emerging as a visible and vulnerable shadow of the "official future" as it threatens to burn its own house to keep the bonfire of progress going.

Ways of making a living and living in place are many and varied in the California North Coast of Little America. A fair example of people I know follows:

Jim and Carolyn Robertson live in the tiny community of Covelo—a hidden valley surrounded by mountains four hours north of San Francisco. They moved there a half-dozen years ago from Sausalito where they had a book designing business and bought a rundown 40 acres and an old cabin in the foothills of Round Valley. In the center of a pasture across from the house they built a simple barnlike structure that one could easily mistake as home for several cows. Instead one enters a spacious workspace filled both with Jim's collection of antique presses and extensive cabinets of typefaces as well as the most modern electronic typesetting equipment. Jim and Carolyn and a small crew design and produce books published by major New York houses from their remote home—and they have won the coveted National Book Award. They work a nine-month year—and devote the summer to their garden, maintenance, and building. Believers in the strength of community, they operate a small but well-stocked book and art supply store in Covelo in addition to doing printing for local businesses.

High in the mountains above Covelo we visited with Tim and Pia McIssac who run 500 cattle on their own land and thousands of acres leased from the Federal Government. Tim grew up in Southern California, although his family has been ranching in Northern California for a hundred years. In this country it takes several hundred acres to support cows, so the McIssac's range stretches for 30 miles along the mountains. During the school year, Pia, a former Italian Olympic skier, and her two teenage sons live in a trailer closer to town so the boys can attend school. They love the remote life although it is changing. Tim says, "people and cattle don't mix." As people build second homes in the remote hills, managing the free ranging herd becomes impossible—the old Western conflict between farmers and fences versus cowboys and cows still exists in these remote hills. Right now the McIssacs make a modest living out of their year-long toil but they are already looking for ways to supplement their income. They are hosting tours for German "cowboys" who fly over for a week of roundup and other old West activities at the ranch. Tim says, "it's amazing. These people spend thousands on western gear and spend their winters riding around an indoor rink in Dusseldorf. They come over here and have a ball."

Ruth Friend pauses from the deliberate rhythm of running the shuttle back and forth on her loom, saying, "What I want to do is make functional fabrics in a traditional manner and be able to make a living at it." From an airy basement studio in Point Reyes Station, Ruth operates Myung Jim Handmade Fabrics (the name given to her by her Korean grandfather) with three helpers. Linen fabrics of her own design use the ancient painstaking Ikat technique which involves wrapping the warp threads to create the pattern, then dying the warp one or more times and then looming the warp into finished fabric with the design expressed in the warp face. After years of mastering the technique, Ruth's fabrics are beginning to attract attention and orders are coming in from showrooms in Los Angeles and San Francisco. She works long hours but finds the work satisfying and quieting. "It's a kind of meditation," she says.

Paul and Anna Hawken and their two young children live in a trailer at Green Gulch Farm, a narrow canyon that winds down to the ocean at Muir Beach, a short distance across the Golden Gate Bridge from San Francisco. Green Gulch is a

monastary and farm operated by the San Francisco Zen Center, a Buddhist community in Northern California. Paul and Anna met some years ago at Findhorn, a spiritually based community in Northern Scotland. Paul, a high school dropout, was one of the founders and former presidents of what is now the largest natural food distributors in the country. He is financial advisor to the Zen Center which operates a number of businesses and recently established a company to import quality English garden tools. He successfully practices his own business and marketing philosophy which is to make available durable, high quality products which enhance simple living. "Living corporations aiming at mass markets are not equipped to fill the many diverse niches in society that want quality." Recently, a major company offered to buy Paul's new company at a handsome price but he and his partner turned them down. In spite of their potential affluence, Paul and Anna live extremely simply, rising at 4:30 a.m. for morning meditation, working on the farm, taking care of the community's children. Several weeks ago, I found them both washing dishes at midnight in the Zen Center's chic restaurant on the San Francisco waterfront.

Stewart Brand's lanky frame rises out of his ancient hand-me-down office chair in the small cluttered cubicle that serves as his office at *CoEvolution Quarterly* and the *Whole Earth Catalog*. "The action is now at the local level. The travel brochures in Europe still urge Europeans to visit Sausalito, a quaint fishing village filled with artists. But what we're becoming is a piece of wall to wall office ghetto. The diversity is disappearing. We need to save it." Brand, who founded the *Whole Earth Catalog* in 1968 as a counterculture information network, only to see it become a million-copy best seller that popped up on every coffee table in fancy suburbs, is passionately committed to the idea of "outlaw communities"—zones where people can live beyond the constraints of routine mass organized society. This he believes is where the cutting-edge of innovation and change tend to occur. Thirty years ago Sausalito *was* a low rent hilly community of artists, fishermen, boat builders, and working people, but the growth of an affluent business-oriented San Francisco, the demand for waterfront cities to berth expensive yachts, and intensive real estate speculation are changing all that. The tightly knit individualistic floating community of houseboats is dissolving, but Brand and others are working at the local political level to work for a plan that will insure room for those who don't live and work in the mainstream.

The people whose livelihood and way of life I've briefly described here are special in some ways but not necessarily unique to the New Age Little America. All are successful, creative, independent, and half are native Californians. All are in their late thirties and early forties and many were active in the great social change movements of the sixties and early seventies.

Another friend observed, "Cleverness in the '80s has replaced 'Crazyness' of the '70s." That "crazyness" was the vision or belief that somehow industrial society could transform and renew itself in a cooperative anarchic nonviolent way through the shamanism of the new music, the interior journey towards a new self, an expanded vision of human potential, the redefinition of what it is to be man or woman, liberatory forms of work, a new fusing of nature and technology; all of this glued together with a spirituality transcending ordinary Western institutionalized religion. Part of the crazyness was that we could *will* the change. That crazyness is still there but it's been put in the closet for the time being. "Cleverness" is adapting to things as they are, yet staying true to the vision and one's own freedom and local community.

In Little America we are looking at those *other* aspects of the environment and learning how to coexist with them. Money, for instance. Some years back a Tibetan Rinpoche or holy man looked at the shining eyes and scruffy faces of the acolytes at his feet and said, "you hippies have a problem. Why do you call money 'bread' when it is money?" And so "right livelihood" is an important issue in a society where money is means as well as end, symbol as well as substance.

Several years ago a "circle of gold" chain letter pyramid scheme swept through coastal Little America and revealed the sad vulnerability of people who in so many other ways had announced their liberation from old values. This hoariest of phony-get-rich quick schemes plays on people's greed and ignorance of the arithmetical reality that for every winner, there must be many losers. Yet the scheme was embraced by many who announced that the money would advance their own as well as their common spirituality. Others announced that "everyone wins, because we all get to play."

In the crazy early phase of revisioning society, the workings and machinery of livelihood and community remained vague, and unformed. Everything would work out. Conflicts could be resolved through encounter groups, "letting it all hang out," letting go of "ego trips." No one would have to make the hard decisions, responsibility could be shared. And all would be united because there was always "them," the others, the dominant society to hold us together in opposition. And the dominant society, powerful yet vulnerable, masking its insecurities and fear through a constant and escalating display of technology and institutionalized violence, was bound to collapse at any moment, leaving out incoherent, unformed, untrained networks to put it all back together again in its new revisioned form. Whatever it was, we could work it out by attention to "process." It hasn't happened yet, thank God, because New Age Little America has a long way to go in its evolution. We are, however, in the second cycle of this evolution. Finding that the vision itself does not make it happen, we are adopting the skills and tools of industrial culture to more discrete finite and healthier purposes.

What seems to be most important to this process is being grounded in a place and committed to living out one's future and close relationships to a specific place. Theoretical architects in the sixties postulated a "plug in" mobile architecture of interchangable parts that would allow one to be at home anywhere on the planet, and to some degree, the vast roving caravans of lumbering "recreational vehicles" and stationary mobile homes which cover most rural landscapes are testimony to the ability of a restless, technologically adept energy-rich society to stay forever on the move, always temporary, never committed to what sustains us. The foremost American paradigm at the moment is the MX missile system where it is proposed to build a vast underground network of roads in which the largest wheeled vehicles on Earth—each carrying a nuclear armed missile— are constantly moving among some 400 launching stations. All this activity is supposed to keep the Russians guessing. As long as we keep moving, we are secure. A parody in the *New Yorker* magazine suggested that the next step would be to create several decoy Americans and put them out in space, keeping them constantly moving in varying orbits.

The MX, like other grand centralized schemes that ignore people's connection and commitment to place, is running into trouble. Government and military planners have learned one important lesson from ecology: If you want to destroy a species all you need do is destroy its habitat. We tried that in Vietnam but ran out of will before we ran out of defoliants. Now, if the national government has its way, energy development and national security will be used to destroy the stubborn independence of ranchers in Wyoming, Native Americans in the southwest states, and regional mindedness of our Northern California coast communities.

We see the danger of an industrial and economic system out of control, a national government that has no genuine ties to the interests of its people. And while we are fearful we are not powerless. Instead of relying on the images and abstractions produced by the system, we rely on our ability to resonate with the natural and social ecology of place to select from the constant linear speeding flow of material productivity and information that which can be adapted to enhance stability, place, and community.

Further Reading: The Seminal Books of the Eighties

Gaia, A Way of Knowing: Political Implications of the New Biology
edited by William Irwin Thompson, 1987

The Ever-Present Origin: Part I, Foundations of the Aperspectival World
by Jean Gebser, 1985

The Gift of Good Land: Further Essays Cultural and Agricultural
by Wendell Berry, 1981

The Seventies: The Environmental Awakening and Response

THE SEVENTIES

The 1970s ushered in a new era. Senator Gaylord Nelson of Wisconsin, an ardent conservationist, had presented to his friend, California Congressman Pete McCloskey, an idea: "Why not have teach-ins about the environment, all over the country?" In 1970, his seed launched Earth Day. The steering committee hired Denis Hayes, a 23-year-old college student, to be the event's organizer. Hayes came to Washington with 20 to 30 college-age kids, and together they sent out newsletters all over the country, to the student body presidents of 10,000 different high schools and a couple of thousand colleges, asking simply, "Would you like to have an Earth Day on April 22?"

In a recent PBS documentary on the birth of Earth Day, Hayes said, "We were trying to create a brand new public consciousness that would cause the rules of the game to change. We had incredible aspirations but there was no World Wide Web; there was no Internet; there was no email; and we had virtually no money … By and large, we created a juggernaut that everyone was willing to embrace, at least stylistically and superficially." (In his 1970 State of the Union Speech, President Nixon embraced environmental reform in a sweeping set of proposals to clean up America's air and water.) The first Earth Day was the largest public demonstration in American history. Events in some cities had half a million people in attendance, and it's estimated that 20 million people participated nationwide.

"We are challenging the ethics of a society," Hayes said, "that with only 6% of the world's population accounts for more than half of its utilization of resources. Our country is stealing from the poorer countries of the world and from generations yet unborn."

After the People's Park episode in Berkeley (see "Building a People's Park," 1969), I had moved my family to a little cabin adjacent to the Point Reyes National Seashore, on the Northern California coast. Traumatized by California Governor Ronald Reagan's violent invasion of Berkeley over the People's Park situation, not to mention the campus administration's unwillingness to challenge the Governor, I told my dean and department chair that I wouldn't teach on the campus for a while. And so we began a quiet new life in the country. But this decade, however stressful, would prove to be perhaps the most productive and eventful of my life.

I began a series of what I called "design thought experiments," the first of which was a class conducted on five acres that I'd purchased, next to the National Park. I called the course "Making a Place in the Country." I was thinking about architecture and design as something larger than designing buildings, but as an integrative design process that considered the basic ecology of space and shelter, sun, soil, water, air, plant and animal life, and wastes as they related to human communities.

"Making A Place in the Country" became a rehearsal for a sequence of three subsequent projects. The first was the construction of an "Energy Pavilion" on the Berkeley campus, an experimental structure that integrated an electricity-generating windmill, a solar food-producing greenhouse with rainwater catchment, and a composting toilet that used no water and returned the finished compost to the greenhouse. Completed just as the 1973 oil embargo woke people up to our dependence on fossil fuels, the Energy Pavilion caught the attention of the media and soon thousands would line up to tour the building. I was told to remove the structure from campus before graduation.

Next, working with a team of ecologists, the nonprofit I'd created called the Farallones Institute, we purchased an old house on the Berkeley Flats and redesigned it as the Integral Urban House (IUH), the next generation of integrative design, combining food production, waste recycling, water reuse, and passive solar heating. A special edition of *Fine Homebuilding* featured IUH as "one of the 25 most important houses built in America since 1620." From there, we moved to an 80-acre abandoned farm and forest site in Sonoma County to start a larger experiment, the Farallones Rural Center, with an educational program that would teach "Whole Systems Design." It's been in operation for 40 years now, the last 20 of which as the Occidental Arts and Ecology Center.

In the fall of 1975, Jerry Brown, the newly elected Governor of California, appointed me as California State Architect, with a mandate to design and build new, energy-efficient and human-centered buildings for the state. We completed a dozen or so major, innovative new buildings, which created real interest in the design and building industries. I also wanted a separate office that would be a "David challenging the Goliath" of bureaucracy and its tendency to resist innovation and new ideas. The Governor obliged, creating an Office of Appropriate Technology, and in that capacity we worked with many state agencies to simplify codes, reduce waste and duplication, and reward local self-reliance in California communities. In 1979, I left Sacramento to return to teaching and practice. I was exhausted.

Bateson Building Dedication, Sacramento, CA, 1979

When I came to Sacramento as California's State Architect, I couldn't see much point to the job unless there was the opportunity to do something. The long hiatus in State construction inherited from the Reagan administration, and the many vacant and run-down blocks of state-owned land in the Capitol area, provided a rich opportunity to rethink and rebuild our State capital in new ways.

A friend with government experience gave me some good advice the first week I was here: "Whatever you're going to do, get it going in your first six months or else you risk not getting anything done at all." The ideas I tried to get going were fairly simple. First was to bring life back into the Capitol area by rehabilitating existing buildings, and adding new affordable housing, community services, and new state office buildings scaled to the neighborhood. The other idea was to build new state buildings that are responsive to people and show the way towards a new architecture that respects its surroundings, its climate, and the cycles of nature.

It has become almost embarrassing to suggest that our government build buildings that people feel good in. Maybe it's because in many people's minds, government has become an affliction and an embarrassment, so why call attention to it? So most government architecture gets designed not by architects but by accountants with red pencils. Most of what gets built is ugly, inhuman, dysfunctional, and because it tends to alienate its inhabitants, no matter how cheap it may appear on the balance sheet, it is terribly expensive in human terms.

In 1975 we had something else going for us and that was the fact that through several generations of seemingly inexhaustible cheap forms of energy, architects and engineers had grown lazy and thoughtless. Buildings were designed with little thought as to where they were located, or how they were oriented. Factors such as natural light, or the daily swings of outside temperature, were not considered as conditions to respond to. So you find the same office buildings or hotels get built in places as different in climate or circumstance as Anchorage, Honolulu, Houston, Bangkok, and Dusseldorf. The result has been an architecture insignificant and indistinguishable around the planet. It has also meant an increasingly expensive waste of precious energy. The average state office building built in the last 20 years requires the equivalent of a gallon of gas each year to provide a comfortable temperature and adequate light for each square foot of space in the building.

The building we are here to dedicate today— the Gregory Bateson State Office Building—reduces that fossil-fuel subsidy by about 75 percent. Over the next 20 years, energy savings alone will repay the cost of the building. There's an added dividend for designing with commonsense energy efficiency.

If we got our energy design act together throughout this country, there would be no need for colossal war budgets to make sure that oil keeps flowing from the rest of a world that is beginning to ask why their resources should pay for the dumb corners we've designed ourselves into.

The press likes to call this building "Solar," that makes for a short, snappy headline. I call it a "climate responsive" building because it recognizes and integrates a variety of characteristics of the local climate into its design. The biggest single user of energy in modern office buildings is lighting. One of the purposes of the atrium we're meeting in today is to bounce daylight into the offices that surround it. The atrium space is actually part of the heating and cooling system for the building. It brings sunlight in to warm the building in the winter and draws heat out of the space in the cool of the summer night. The concrete mass of the building acts like a battery—storing heat on cold days, and storing cool night air on warm days.

I want to add some thoughts about Gregory Bateson in whose memory this building is dedicated. Gregory was a mentor to myself and to Governor Jerry Brown. Most of Gregory's life was spent trying to illuminate the wholeness that is in man and the natural world. We are all part of what Gregory called, "the pattern which connects," which is the form of life itself. Gregory's search led in many directions: the function of language and thought, the nature of human cultures, biology and the connections among living things. Because he cut through the familiar habits of mind that cloud our everyday vision, he was not always easy to understand. To hear what he was saying—and he often talked not science but stories—meant replacing a lot of what you thought you knew. In the last month of his life, I asked him what single thing was needed for people to grasp a new way of looking at their world. He said, "People are mad for quantity, yet what is significant is quality and difference."

And so it is in this building named in honor of Gregory Bateson. We found that in designing around natural energy flows, we became sensitive to difference. The measure became not foot-candles of quantifiable illumination, but the quality of light you actually experience. We found we could consider the wall of the building not as a static two-dimensional architectural element, but as a living skin that is sensitive to and adapts to differences in temperature and light. We found out that designing a building that saves energy, means designing a building that is sensitive to differences and results in a building that people felt more comfortable in. We humans are not designed to live and work at temperatures and lighting that are uniform and constant. We feel most alive when we experience subtle cycles of difference in our surroundings. This building named in his honor itself becomes, "the pattern which connects" us to the change and flow of climate, season, sun and shadow, constantly tuning our awareness of the natural cycles that support all life.

Perhaps this is what esthetics and beauty are all about. Perhaps what we find beautiful is that which connects us to an experience of difference—to an experience of the patterns of wholeness which distinguish the living world for the works of Man.

"Ecotopia Now: Utopia Brought Down to Earth," *New Age*, 1979

About the same time a few years ago, two different visionary statements first appeared in print: Gerard O'Neill's proposal to create self-sufficient human colonies in outer space, and Amory Lovins's scenario for a frugal society driven by decentralized, renewable energy sources.

O'Neill's proposal, published in *CoEvolution Quarterly*, follows in the footsteps of classic utopian planning. The idea captures the imagination by its very outrageousness, presented in a series of slick, full-color illustrations of what life could be like out there at L-5. These powerful images are followed up by other concept drawings and diagrams. It is a fantasy of what technology might be able to do if we have sufficient will, daring, and money to try the almost-impossible. The Space Colony concept has attracted a lot of adherents among influential and creative people, as well as considerable interest from the major military hardware suppliers.

Lovins's proposal, first published in the staid journal *Foreign Affairs* and then republished by Friends of the Earth in its magazine *Not Man Apart* (it's now available as a book, *Soft Energy Paths*), is a vision of a very different sort. For one thing, it is not articulated with drawings or diagrams or any physical image of the future. What Lovins does is build a carefully reasoned case for how the industrialized world can grow into the next century, maintaining a high material standard of living, while radically decreasing its dependence on fossil fuel-derived forms of energy. In making his case, Lovins relies heavily on the numbers produced by the heavy technology establishment, and in a great act of one-upmanship he beats the enemy at their own game. In suggesting more efficient technologies and extrapolating the benefits we would derive from them, Lovins sticks to proven examples that are now at work somewhere in the world and for which cost figures and performance data are available.

Both of these proposals created quite a stir, and they continue to do so, both at the level of national policy and in the hearts and minds of many people who have been touched by them. Congress seriously considered putting lots of money into space colonies, and although the Carter administration seems to have shelved the idea for the moment, the space colony people continue the dialogue and even have their own magazine.

Soft Energy Paths has been a seminal manifesto, spawning the strategy of a national energy policy built on the use of conservation techniques and solar-based, decentralized technologies; however, results have been limited thus far. The "big bang for a buck" mega-technologists still are setting our national energy policy, determining priorities and deciding where the money will go. David has not yet popped Goliath with that lethal stone.

But my story is not so much about either of these

proposals. It is about what I've learned from them and how it applies to an aspect of the future as I see it. When space colonies and soft energy paths came into flower, I was in Sacramento serving as California State Architect and first director of the newly created Office of Appropriate Technology. I was thought to have some power, because I had relatively free rein over a rather large building program and because, as a person with ideas, I had ample opportunity to talk with the governor.

Friends brought Amory Lovins over to my apartment. I found him a wry, quick fellow, diffident and confident at the same time. He showed me the draft of the piece he was working on for *Foreign Affairs*. I was impressed with how he had pieced many pieces together, but the part that Amory was most excited about—the numbers, the quads of energy saved in his scenario—went past me. I have never seen a quad of energy (a quadrillion BTU [British thermal unit]), nor can I imagine it. It is as unknown and mysterious to me as the quark so dear to the more esoteric physicists. I like to be able to see what people are talking about, to give it form in my mind; numbers alone hold very limited form, and thus excitement, for me. But, even if Amory's work lacked specifics of form so close to my architect's heart, I could sense the great impact that it could have—and, to my surprise and delight, has had.

The space colonies concept first burst on the scene in the form of a full-color cover on *CoEvolution Quarterly*. Within days I started getting calls about how Stewart had sold out or gone absolutely bananas. Having known Stewart since the *Whole Earth Catalog*'s early days, I wouldn't hold either charge against him, since he doesn't fit such conventional categories. I was puzzled, though, by all the interest that the idea elicited: I have never read any work of science fiction (although I've tried many times), and when "we" made it to the moon, I had no desire to watch it on TV. As with the takeoff of Lovins's ideas, the success of the space colonies concept was a surprise for me—at the time not a pleasant one. As I studied the issue, I found myself getting annoyed, and as space colony talk escalated, I found myself getting angry. What bothered me was that so much careful attention had gone into a world of fantasy that people might confuse with something actually worth doing. And then I got angry when I realized what power the drawings and the image had for many people.

What conclusions do I draw from the success of these two concepts?

1. Our need for images of the future is strong.
2. The image is stronger in proportion to our ability to visualize a real place.
3. For a variety of reasons, architects and planners have ceased providing these images, perhaps because few believe that they can be realized in today's world. (When I complained to Governor Brown that it took 68 separate permits from a myriad of jurisdictions to be allowed to farm edible fish in public streams, he replied "Sure, that's why space colonies—no permits.") In space, planning is necessary and respectable; here it is practically impossible. So utopian thinking has migrated into science fiction and outer space.
4. A decentralized technologically intelligent society, based on renewable sources of energy, is possible, as Lovins and others have shown. But most people don't believe it, and won't believe it until they are shown, through actual examples that they can touch, feel, and experience. People will move to a conserving way of life, not out of guilt or expedience, but because it feels better and is more satisfying. As Bucky Fuller observed long ago, people change when they are shown physical alternatives.

REVITALIZING THE URBAN ENVIRONMENT

The image of a self-sufficient way of life in balance with nature has always been presented as an alternative that can only be realized in the country and through a rural economy. But we have the means right now to design a sustainable, ecologically sound pattern into the compact urban context. We can build new communities that integrate available technologies with ecological principles to produce a high quality of urban life that is sustainable without the use of the nonrenewable resources.

Realizing this goal will require some important shifts in how we live and in the design of our urban life support systems. The values that are inherent in such shifts are steadily gaining ground in this country. In the long run our choice will be to adapt our cities and suburbs toward ecological stability or to abandon them. First, we need to build some models from scratch to show that the goal can be realized, and that it is worth doing. The major features of the Ecotopian city include:

- Bringing home and workplace closer together, in a decentralized mode, thus reducing the need for extensive use of private autos to a fraction of today's use and cutting down not only energy use but the insatiable demand of the autoculture for space (30–50 percent of the land area in our cities and suburbs is given over to cars). Reducing cars and streets makes possible a compact human-scale environment where much of what is today asphalt can be used productively.
- Bringing food production and processing into the home, neighborhood, and region, thus reducing dependency on an energy-intensive, land-exploitative food system.
- Generating electricity locally from the sun and from biomass, and employing it selectively for its best uses: mechanical energy and lighting.
- Bringing water use in balance with locally available, sustainable supplies, through conservation and recycling.
- Returning all organic wastes to the soil.
- Designing all buildings so that they are integrally heated and cooled by the action of sun and local climate (this is feasible in most parts of the country year-round).

Incorporating these features, it is possible to forge a pattern that retains the best of the high-technological, urban, information-oriented culture, while renewing people's sense of place and their connection to the basic rituals involved in an active participation in the natural cycles of the earth.

Traditionally, cities have always been thought of and designed as dense human settlements that require a vast hinterland for their support. In the orthodox view, the city is seen as a transformer where the vast bounty of natural systems is converted into the capital savings of civilization, in the form of cultural information and material products. In other words, cities are conceived of as machines—indeed, inefficient and inelegant machines for living. Raw materials move through them as quickly as possible. Some fuel the machine itself; some are transformed into products and information; and most are wasted.

In contrast is the natural system, in which materials flow in a continuous cycle or loop, and energy is extracted at each level. The result is a balanced system, driven by the energy of the sun and transformed by the diverse strategies devised through evolution.

The idea of designing a city around ecological balance is not new. Seventy years ago Britain's Ebenezer Howard diagrammed "garden cities" ringed by agricultural and open space zones. The garden cities were linked together with mass transit, and movement within the city was by foot or bicycle, with a maximum travel time to workplace of 15 minutes. In the 1930s Frank Lloyd Wright presented his utopian plan, called "Broadacre City": the dense center of the megalopolis was dismantled into a horizontal city, where each family had its own home and space to grow food—an organic version of the suburbs that were to follow.

These and other earlier utopian proposals were visionary responses to the growing tide of urbanization. High population density was seen as a destabilizing force, because it would lead to domination by large, alienating institutions and to the loss of a direct connection with the land, nature, and the food supply.

Even more significant than population density today is energy density, or the quantity of resources—per unit area—that must be imported to maintain the life of any community. Chances are, the greater the quantity of imported resources needed to support life, the greater the ecological damage and social instability in the community.

Urban cultures will probably survive as long as humanity survives. The challenge, then, is to design ecologically balanced communities—ideally, where little or no nonrenewable resources need to be imported into the community for its maintenance and survival. Since most of the technologies and systems that now maintain modern urban life are dependent on one-time-use fossil fuels, the trick will be to merge the built environment with nature; to design new systems that will harmonize with, amplify, and harvest the products of natural cycles in the environment; and to transform solar energy into forms capable of powering modern society. This task will require the highest level of both scientific and esthetic understanding, if not wisdom—which is, after all, an understanding of events in their total context.

Our understanding of how to translate ecological principles into the design of buildings, neighborhoods, cities, and towns is only just beginning, and creative solutions will depend on the fruitful marriage of disciplines—biology and ecology on the one side, architecture and engineering on the other—that today rarely communicate with one another. Architects and planners are not expected to know anything about ecology, and biologists—with the rare exception of activists such as Barry Commoner or Paul Ehrlich—stay in the laboratories, or in the field. Those people who actually shape our cities and our futures—the politicians, senior bureaucrats, businesspeople, developers, financiers—come out of law and business schools, speaking another language. Yet it is their decisions and visions—or lack of vision—that will decide our future.

TRANSLATING LINEAR TO ECOLOGICAL

A brief comparison of the differences between an ecological system and the linear, machinelike system that is typical of today's urban pattern might be useful. The properties of a linear system, and their ecological equivalents, exist along a continuum. We need to get a feeling for when a particular design approaches the linear and when it approaches the ecological.

A Systems Spectrum

Linear System	Ecological System
Energy flows in straight lines	Energy flows in loops
Made up of components with separate, specialized functions	Made up of components with overlapping functions
High entropy, low information	Low entropy, high information
Memory stored in centralized, specialized components	Memory stored in all components
High rate of energy flow and material loss	Low rate of energy flow and material loss

Linear System	Ecological System
Single channels for energy flow	Multiple channels for energy flow
High waste and pollution: resources out of place	No waste: the output of one channel is input for another

In brief, ecological systems incorporate four basic principles:

1. Materials and energy are processed through closed loops and webs of multiple channels.
2. Energy is released within the system, in small increments.
3. A steady rate is maintained through information passed through the permeable boundaries between systems.
4. Information is stored in a decentralized, genetic memory.

Some of these principles are illustrated in the Farallones Integral Urban House. In the Integral House, each major functional system employs multiple pathways for material and energy flow. The heating system, for example, includes direct solar gain through windows, a solar air space-heating system, and a woodstove heater for cloudy cold days. Organic waste can be shunted in a variety of ways. Human fecal matter decomposes in a composting toilet and, when fully decomposed, is used as a soil amendment for ornamental plants. Urine is collected and used as a nitrogen-rich fertilizer. Kitchen scraps are fed to the chickens and thus converted into edible protein; the chicken manure is recycled in the garden. Garbage can also be composted or fed into worm cultures to make a nutrient-rich casting for garden use; the worms are then fed to the chickens or the fish in the pond. Duckweed in the pond absorbs toxic fish waste and in turn is dried and fed to the chickens. These are all examples of multiple loops.

An important feature of the multiple pathway is that each component in such a system tends to perform overlapping functions. Thus, one test of the integral quality of any system is the extent to which components are integrated into multiple functions. An electric heater can only be an electric heater. A garbage truck can only be a garbage truck. However, windows admit light, provide a view, and can also act as a solar collector. An attached greenhouse can be a solar collector and a storage system, a place to grow seedlings and winter vegetables, or a location for a hot tub. A planting box, however small, together with composting buckets, can take the place of a smelly garbage can and noisy garbage truck; besides processing waste nutrients, it provides a source of beauty, foods, flowers, and can be the focus for many pleasant leisure hours.

The system of multiple pathways is closely linked to the idea of the diversity and stability of healthy, natural systems, and the multiple pathway is an interactive process within any food or nutrient chain. For example, in a healthy garden, a diversity of plants will ensure that there is going to be a diversity in insect life associated with those plants: thus, one insect population is not likely to get out of control and become a pest. The use of pesticides, on the other hand, is a positive feedback cycle: to devote the entire Midwest to one crop, such as corn, is to foster a predator that gets totally out of control; then pesticide is used, but the insects become resistant, and it becomes necessary to continue to apply more and more pesticide. Slowly, learning from its mistakes, agriculture is beginning to take the principle of diversity into account.

The linear mode is particularly inefficient in dealing with waste and garbage. Waste is simply hauled to land-fills, and most urban areas are running out of available land-fill areas: cities are being forced to haul garbage to remote locations hundreds of miles away. Human waste is diluted in the ratio of 100 to 1 with potable water and piped to large sewage factories, where the solids are removed through mechanical and bacterial action; the nutrient-rich effluent that remains is dumped into rivers or the ocean, where it overloads the ability of natural systems to provide oxygen needed by the organisms in the effluent. There results a condition known as eutrophication, and a surge of microbiological and algae growth depletes the oxygen and fouls up the water. (For a more complete description of the modern sewage scandal and some alternatives, see my book *The Toilet Papers*.)

The concept of flow is crucial. Ecological design tends to rely on smaller, more decentralized units, to reduce the overall flow, and thus to reduce energy use. As a rule, in any ecologically designed system, the total energy flow required will be less than that in the linear system. In linear systems, energy pulses through in order to achieve maximum product flow, with a high rate of waste. The use of electricity to heat a house is a prime example: more times the amount of energy in high quality fuels is consumed than will finally result in useful heat in the home. The way we heat our homes with electricity—particularly that provided by nuclear power—is equivalent to "using a chainsaw to cut butter." Moreover, the economic costs are not borne by the immediate user but get buried in the increasing entropy of larger systems. With nuclear electricity, the costs are buried in the entire rate base, and consumers generally don't know what they're paying for.

Modern agriculture is another energy sink: it uses far more energy to produce food than it takes out. In traditional agriculture that ratio is reversed. In the U.S. it takes 20 to 30 calories of energy to produce 1 calorie of food; in China it takes 1 calorie of energy (mostly human) to produce 30 calories of food. The agribusiness approach is rationalized on the basis that the total productivity of energy-intensive agriculture is far higher than traditional methods, and that we would starve without it: if the fossil-fuel subsidy were removed, food prices would be astronomical. With our food system so dependent on energy waste, that claim is all too sadly true.

PROTOTYPES AND PROGRESS

Through the careful orchestration of food, and nutrient chains integrated with land use and the design of human space, we can begin to create systems with multiple functions, each using the products of the other, wasting nothing; we can make sure that functions overlap so that should one system fail, others may take its place. This type of design is distinctly unlinear and nonstatic: its esthetic grows, not out of the arbitrary and increasingly foolish dictates of architectural fashion, but out of the dynamic and functional interplay of living systems in harmony with human needs.

The concept of designing and constructing new communities around the principles of ecological stability and energy efficiency is slowly gaining ground. Most of the innovation I'm familiar with has come from committed individuals and small struggling groups, rather than from the corporation or established research factories. Beginning in the early 1970s, a number of groups began to design, construct, and experiment with various forms of habitation. The best-known continuing examples are New Alchemy's Arks—first at Woods Hole, Massachusetts, then on Prince Edward Island in Canada—and Farallones Institute's Integral Urban House in Berkeley, California. New Alchemy's experiments have concentrated on growing plants and fish in greenhouse-type spaces; the Prince Edward Island greenhouse incorporates space for a residence as well. In Berkeley, the Farallones experiment began with an 80-year-old derelict Victorian house which was remodeled into a continuing experiment; it serves to show how the single family urban dwelling and lot can be transformed into a place that minimizes the need to import food and energy,

and to export waste and pollution. (The Farallones experiment, with its implications for homes across the country, has now been documented in a book *The Integral Urban House*.)

The significance of these experiments is their focus on the connections among the systems that make up a house, and their insistence on seeing the design of habitation and human space as fundamentally a question of biological design. These rudimentary projects started on a small scale not only because limited funding has a way of keeping things small, but because the individual habitation is an obvious place to start. These very modest beginnings, however, have been conceived from the outset as the first step toward a larger vision of organically whole and balanced communities.

Paolo Soleri comes immediately to mind as someone whose canvas started out vast, with visions of what he termed "Arcologies"—massive structures housing thousands. However, Soleri's plans have evolved over the years—influenced, I think, by the work of biologically oriented people working at a smaller scale, and by the slow pace of Arcostanti construction, which allows Soleri and his associates to learn and evolve the concept as they build. The new "Arcologies" feature greenhouses cascading down austere canyons, as well as water and waste recycling systems. He has also begun to study the thermodynamics of heat transfer to provide for solar heating and cooling.

Of all the emerging technologies that fit into an ecological design, solar heating and cooling of buildings is the one that has captured the most public attention, as well as the imagination of architects and builders. Since the heating and cooling of buildings accounts for some 40 percent of our nonrenewable energy use, that interest is well placed.

The type of solar systems that show the most promise so far are those misleadingly labeled as "passive"; that is, the system is designed as part of the building and its functions, as opposed to "active" systems which involve solar machinery added on to the structure. Integral solar design makes use of, and combines, many commonsense design principles, such as proper orientation, shading and placement of landscaping, and especially the use of the building's mass as a thermal battery to store heat or "coolth."

In the past several years, the concept of the solar greenhouse has gained favor, since they can be added onto existing buildings as well as designed as part of new structures. In this concept, a south-facing greenhouse, combined with storage mass in its walls or in a sunken rockbed, catches and stores heat, which is then distributed to the rest of the building. And of course the greenhouse serves not only as part of the solar system, but as a place to grow plants, and is a usable room. In locations such as the Midwest, with its dry winters, a greenhouse equipped with a hot tub, wood-stove, and planting area could not only serve as part of a heating system (with the hot tub contributing to the heat storage system), it could change the whole interior climate and psychology of the house, providing needed humidity, winter salads, and pleasurable space.

Experiments that try to create biologically stable habitats by integrating various technologies on a small scale can, of course, be only part of the answer. I have never liked the bomb shelter mentality connected to some people's idea of self-sufficiency. The goal is to reduce dependency and centralization where possible, but in the end our well-being is tied to the local networks that we create.

Accordingly, many people are now working hard to develop and test specific technologies that can come together to form an integrated life support system at the community scale. A balanced community should be able to grow most of its own food in its backyards and on the block, with the rest coming from the immediate region; any organic wastes generated through food production and use can be returned to the soil to maintain fertility. Thus, the basic building block in designing biologically stable human settlements may be the development of simple, small-scale, intensive agricultural techniques that can be used by the average urban person and small farmers.

In a garden covering several acres in a Palo Alto industrial park, former Yale systems analyst John Jeavons has for some years been quietly and methodically developing what he calls a "mini-farm": plots of 1/10 acre which, he calculates, could produce $10,000–20,000 worth of vegetables with one person working a 40-hour week eight months of the year. Each 2,800-square-foot plot should, he estimates, provide a balanced year-round diet for one person, including grain (wheat was heating up on the December day we visited), vegetables, and fruit (dwarf fruit trees are interplanted in the beds). Jeavons claims that one person could tend such a plot in a half-hour per day, using one-hundredth of the fossil fuel that today's agriculture would devote to that area, and one-eighth the water.

A shift from diversified massive monoculture type agriculture to local intensive agriculture would result in substantial water savings across the board, since agribusiness uses 90 percent of our water (often with federal subsidy) and uses it extremely wastefully.

High-quality water is rapidly becoming a scarce resource in many parts of the country. At its price, though, it is still a best buy: What else can you purchase, delivered in your home, for pennies per ton? In parts of the country, particularly the western Sunbelt, water is being mined and used up much like any other nonrenewable resource, and natural underground reservoirs, which take hundreds of years to build up, are being depleted at alarming rates.

When we were planning the Farallones Rural Center, one of our goals was to demonstrate the potential for low water use in water-short rural areas. The authorities in the county initially refused us permits on the basis that we must be able to supply and dispose of 150 gallons per person per day, which is the accepted standard for water use. We were able to get by with about a tenth of that for domestic use. Since then, necessity—in the form of recurrent droughts in California—has spurred an interest in water-conserving technologies, and even the affluent folks in Marin County were able to reduce their water consumption by 60 percent without any change in technology.

The prevalent suburban pattern in the United States could be easily adapted to save even more energy, by being converted to intensive garden production of the sort promoted by Jeavons. The 19 million acres of suburban lawns in this country are major consumers of pesticides and fertilizers; if they were converted to mini-farms, they could, according to Jeavons's productivity figures, feed this country!

Removing redundant streets would add many millions more of farmable acres in our spread-out cities. Most of our cities and suburbs are built on flat, alluvial plains, and the soil is often the best there is. Many agriculturists seem skeptical of Jeavons's figures, but it is clear from his work and that of others—including the Farallones gardeners—that the intensively planted, raised-bed approach to urban farming is capable of producing year-round crops in limited space with far greater yields and less care than conventional methods. For most Americans, tending a small intensive garden would mean one less TV show a day, and some more time off their duff—not a bad tradeoff.

When food and home are brought closer together, the cycle of waste is reduced. Kitchen garbage can be composted and returned to the soil. Collecting human wastes in waterless composting toilets allows us to return these otherwise wasted nutrients to the soil, and so the cycle of water waste and sewage pollution can be broken.

There are many other technologies that might be used in an Ecotopian community. The Solar Aquacell system, developed by a group of young San Diego marine biologists, removes the nutrients

from sewage in closed greenhouses, using water hyacinths—a rapidly growing plant whose floating root system soaks up nutrients. Edible seafood, such as giant prawns, can also be cultivated. Composted or dried, the hyacinths make an excellent cattle feed.

During my time in Sacramento, I introduced this innovative and cost-effective technology to bureaucrats and engineers building new energy-intensive mega-sewage plants. Even without the support of state or federal funds, the town of Hercules, California, has decided to build a 4-million-gallon-a-day Solar Aquacell plant. The main drawback of this biologically sound system is that more space is required for the plant, since sewage is retained for a week instead of a few hours. The greatest asset of the Aquacell system is that water purified by this fully biological process is of such high quality that it can be used for recreation or irrigation.

Left to its own devices, standard development intensifies water problems. In the typical suburb, more than half the surface area is covered with streets, driveways, and roofs that do not retain water. The result is a massive run-off that overpowers the holding capacity of native streams, which then become the subject of concrete "stabilization" programs. Now communities such as Monterey County, California, are considering requiring that homes install old-fashioned cisterns to contain run-off and to store rain water for use in the dry season.

All of the technologies discussed so far could be implemented in our existing communities without causing major social disruption and change. They are transitional technologies; they create the basis for a sustainable society. However, one radical, obvious, and difficult change remains: the segregation in time and space of workplace from homeplace, and our total dependence on the automobile—the production, care, and feeding of which consumes around 40 percent of our natural resources and the lion's share of the world's depletable energy supplies.

Fly low over any major city and suburban area, and you will begin to get a full picture of how the automobile dominates the use of land. Not until people can see an alternative that works, is the pattern likely to change. In the Ecotopian community, the road system must be designed so that cars cannot be used for short trips, and work locations must be scattered throughout the community, to reduce auto commuting.

Some people seem to think that our unique purpose as a species is to release all the hydrocarbons from underneath the earth's surface and then go the way of the dinosaur. If this is the case, then the internal combustion engine and the automobile fill an important ecological niche toward our own destruction.

THE NEW ESTHETICS

Without esthetics, neither economy nor efficiency of energy have any meaning. Esthetics is conceptual information and varies from culture to culture: It is the meaning that we find in form. The meaning that we derive from any environment is limited by the form of that environment. Our interactions with complex and diverse living systems increase our awareness and add to the meaning that we derive from life.

Our spirits are enriched and constantly recharged by our functional and ritualistic connections to the natural world. The preindustrial esthetic was always based on that kind of connection. Whether evidenced in the miniature garden found in each home in a dense Japanese neighborhood, or the simple Arab courtyard fountain, or the shade elms of New England commons, the whole picturesque "architecture without architects" of the earlier world adapted habitat to local materials, site, climate, and ecosystem.

The importance of esthetics is the kind of

participation that it brings about with natural systems. It is from this relationship that the new esthetics must be derived. For the most part, however, Americans have lost that intimate connection and an awareness of their place in the natural world. The "natural" aspect has been reduced to empty symbols, such as the tract house lawn, which started out as a sheep meadow—the lawn was there for sheep to crop. Ecosystems have become dim landscapes to be appreciated out of car windows—low-information media like TV screens.

The task, then, of ecological design, is to begin to recreate the opportunities for people to derive meaning and satisfaction from their experience with natural cycles.

CONSCIOUS COMMUNITY

The model of the Ecotopian city need not be built all of a piece. It need not involve a radically different process from the way communities get planned and built today. The critical aspect is the disposition of land, building guidelines, and the design of life support systems.

The Bible tells us that "Without vision the people perish." Today people seem to be without a shared positive vision of what the future could be; indeed, the polls continually tell us that the future looks bleak to most Americans. Everything seems to have become unmanageable. Thus, a concern for the collective environment, outside of neighbors and friends, has been replaced by the urge for self-improvement, if not plain self-indulgence. The future is nowhere to be found.

Meanwhile, every eight weeks the equivalent of a new city for 400,000 people gets built in this country—an extension of the existing pattern. The cities continue to rot, essential services deteriorate, and the thin mantle of soil, water, air, and biotic life that is the true basis for our affluence continues to be assaulted, out of ignorance and greed.

The overall picture is not so unremittingly grim as current trends might seem to suggest. Ecotopian communities are possible *right now*, and the construction of some modest first examples might help to restore some of our lost hope. Visionary eco-designers need to join forces with number-crunching analysts and can-do engineers to create prototypes. Our more enlightened entrepreneurs and politicians need to commit themselves to an idea that could bring some much-needed credit to a system whose concern for human and environmental values seems to be at a cynical new low point.

The seeds of ecological design *are* beginning to sprout, however, and many of the hardware components to create an ecologically stable urban community have already been developed and are working. What we have yet to do is bring together all the threads and weave them into a single coherent design for a new community.

"The Coming Age of Natural Design,"
L'Architecture d'Aujourd'hui, March 1975

In architecture, monumentality is most often confused with substance. Any object, sufficiently enlarged in size, becomes architecture. Claes Oldenburg, sensing that our symbols today lie in the realm of the man-made, has shown that any common object may be elevated to monument simply by puffing up its scale. Unfortunately, our leading architects, whose ego and belief in bigness may outweigh their common sense, have largely succumbed to this false dream.

Bigness is also often confused with complexity. Structures that termites construct with their own feces incorporate a highly sophisticated means of climatic adaptation and circulation unequaled by the mammoth megastructures of today. The problem is that while we have mastered many aspects of the physical sciences, the design of the built environment does not take into account the complexity of life support, the delicate web of ecosystemic processes that make a place livable. For me, there is only one architecture worth trying to master, and that is architecture connected to life process, or what we can call "Natural Design," architecture with a small "a."

Large "A" Architecture confuses bigness with substance and complexity. Large "A" Architecture exists to symbolize the power of centralized bureaucracy, technology, and economics; in short, "Progress." It has no process to take into account the complexity, richness, and diversity of Life.

The main function of architecture in this century has been to provide the settings and armature for the techno-fantasies of modern industrial culture. Modern architecture has glorified man over nature, organization and technology over man. For 50 years, architects have been spurred on by the logical–positivist visions of the Futurists, and now having come so far towards realizing these once fantastic visions we discover that in our dream state we helped build a hollow nightmare.

Progress created the illusion that man and his machines were no longer dependent on Nature. Human will and intelligence should reshape Earth into a limitless cornucopia. Architecture was called into service by this new game. Design became a process of abstracting reality into numbers and relationships.

What we call "progress" is paid for from an Earth savings account that will be empty in a few short decades. Every aspect of our modern industrial urbanized way of life is dependent on hydrocarbons—a gift from the steamy jungles of many millions of years ago. Architects, engineers, and planners have until recently taken these energy sources largely for granted. The archetypal environments of the fossil-fuel age—massive cities and high-rise buildings—will soon be as obsolete as the dinosaurs that roamed the forests since turned to oil.

The continuing base for an advanced post-progress civilization is the ability of diverse natural ecosystems to capture and fix solar radiation into usable forms of energy. By recognizing our deep dependence on the subtle and self-healing processes of nature, we are offered sustenance as well as independence and autonomy. An advanced society centered on a stable solar economy will combine a highly developed scientific understanding with a liberating technology. None of this need be bought at the expense of a return to human slavery and drudgery. Modern China, in some sense, shows the way. Perhaps for once, while East follows West, *West may follow East*, and where they meet there is a future.

Progress continues as a powerful game, even today sweeping new millions along the path to material magic. Like a storm at the peak of its fury, the center is a vacuum; the structure collapses from its center on out. So it is not surprising that the United States, the first country to most fully be subjected to the trauma of full-scale industrialization, is also the first Western country where a significant number of people are looking to develop a saner, more stable, and ecologically sound and humanly responsive technology.

In the United States, perhaps beginning around the time of the assassination of John F. Kennedy and the fall of Camelot, the feeling that centrist culture no longer had the answers began to intensify and move through broad reaches of the culture. It was a view reinforced by the failures of liberal politics, culminating in the civil rights struggles and Vietnam, the growing evidence of ecological and environmental disasters, the cancerous suburbanization and the failure to achieve significant social or physical renewal in the cities. One can only guess about the agents that catalyzed the process of perceiving the unreal. Certainly the wide use of marijuana and psychedelics in the mid-sixties was a powerful tool but in itself did not provide the means to another place.

Where were models for another way? We are still looking, but the first tentative steps have been taken these last years. For many it was a connection to the sand, the securing of an independent base for themselves away from the technological dependencies of the city. Nothing new in this, except that, carried out in large enough numbers, it may represent a reversal of what planners have solemnly announced as "inevitable:" the continued flow of rural populations into ever-larger urban centers. Many thousands of young people in the U.S. are trying to make a self-sufficient life for themselves in abandoned rural areas, despite the many ways in which official policy discourages the small independent farming unit and subsidizes huge-scale corporate farming. Only in Norway—that I know of—does government subsidize the small family farm, believing in its innate positive social and environmental value.

But twentieth-century homesteading is a tough business, requiring lots of discipline, resourcefulness, and knowledge—not for masses of people at this point. Its psychological effect, amplified through media such as the *Whole Earth Catalog*, *Mother Earth News*, *Organic Gardening and Farming*, is significant in offering up the possibility for many people of becoming a competent and independent generalist while leading a fulfilling life. It is hard to dismiss someone's life as "romantic" and "escapist" when you are eating food they have grown in a house they have built out of materials they have gathered. Perhaps that is why many "practical" people in the centrist culture don't bother to confirm their children's experience. Indeed, it is amusing that the very people who often deride such experience as

"impractical, romantic, and escapist" are very often the same people who will jet around the Earth in search of a quiet beach in an unspoiled place, where they pay thousands of dollars just to sit, and to the puzzlement of the local natives.

My guess is that a large proportion of the professional community is dissatisfied with what they must see as a way of life that, while perhaps meeting their gross material needs, has betrayed whatever visions and promise they once may have had. In architecture this seems particularly true. All of us who have practiced know that architecture is a business that serves corporate interests and the state, yet its underlying themes still maintain its connection to the humanistic, nature-centered power of the individual artist–creator. The deaths of the great makers of the modern movement—Gropius, Le Corbusier, Mies, and Wright—and the failure of the international architectural establishment to produce anyone of their stature, has tended to leave the profession and its training grounds in the university schools of architecture without any powerful figures to represent a happy marriage of humanistic idealism and technological prowess.

Bernard Rudofsky's *Architecture Without Architects* popularized architecture's source in indigenous, organic habitation that pre-industrial cultures habitually produced. However, imitation misses the point.

Reproducing Mediterranean fishing villages or Northern California wood barns as stage sets for vacations with good taste is style without substance. To extol the virtues of Las Vegas or Los Angeles as expressions of "popular" design is to cynically ignore the powerful political and economic interests who are the real authors of these landscapes.

The point is so obvious that it is hard to keep hold of it: consistency, beauty, naturalness, and order in architecture are not attributes of form alone; they are simply expressions of values, a way of life and a process. Any assessment of form is always an assessment of culture and value. Architecture is a mirror of the society that creates it; how we, in turn, assess that architecture reflects our own values.

The socially conscious architect is in a schizophrenic place. As a technician, he serves processes and purposes that often destroy and inhibit organic and natural design by people, themselves.

Two important books in recent years illustrate the point through the personal, sometimes agonizing, experience of the authors. In *Freedom to Build*, a group of American housing experts involved in various low-cost housing schemes, here and abroad, reach a consensus that the housing schemes of architects and bureaucrats are seldom as workable and economic as what people can do for themselves with the same resources. The Egyptian architect, Hassan Fathy, in *Architecture for the Poor*, recounts his long experience with trying to reestablish an Earth architecture in Egypt, in the end to be defeated by the housing bureaucracy that favors more "advanced" Western ways. We have seen the pattern all over the world: pleasing, effective, and economical indigenous habitat skills and processes destroyed and replaced with mass sterility.

Architects, no matter how well intentioned, are almost inevitably agents for destruction of natural process wherever they encounter it. How could it be otherwise, when Western technology, centralization, economics, and progress are the gods that must be served?

Faced with this dilemma five years ago, I left private practice and set about to build a house in the country for my family and myself. It seemed the appropriate learning experience and therapy for me, after spending ten years designing places for other people. The process of building and living in the first house I built, and the one that soon followed, revealed the true connectedness of architecture to the rest of life. It exposed my deep ignorance of many practical matters, as well as the disordered image of who I thought I was.

A friend remarked that houses are museums to one's past, and I find this very true. When one *designs*, one freezes an image, and always it is of the past. And always it is an *image*, an abstraction, and a commitment to a form that is a commitment to particular values. Creating a form for one's own life and designing the physical container is a deep, sometimes satisfying, sometimes terrifying experience. And ultimately the image and the form are a mirror, but always of time that has already passed.

I do not feel that either of the houses I have made for us is very successful. They can be no better than the sum of my life architecture, and I find I have more to learn each day, but it cannot be hurried. Each day is the teacher—in its own way.

Although some of my friends who have built their own houses are architecturally trained, most are not. The most inspiring, beautiful, and practical places reflect the order, integrity, skills, energy, knowledge, and imagination—in short, *the life space*—of their builders. Architectural training seems to have little to do with the results. Indeed, most of the architect–builders I know feel they have had to *unlearn* most of the fixed images they so assiduously developed over the years. Certainly this has been true for me. Knowledge of details, drawing visualization, and engineering are the skills of most value; all those pretty pictures in the magazines and volumes on spatial concepts are positively harmful to practical creation.

In this part of the country, there are many people following the path of building for themselves. Our situation in Northern California is not typical of the U.S.

In a rapidly changing world of more people, less resources, absurd waste, and abject poverty, it makes sense to get down to basics, to simplify, to get in touch with what it takes to support your own view of what you take to be "reality."

We first developed tools to modify the natural environment in order to enhance our chances for survival. Architecture grows out of this primary physiological and biological need, which has in time been overshadowed by other requirements. In the short space of a few hundred years, our tools, monstrously swollen by a fossil-fuel diet, threaten to overwhelm our sensibility and Nature's capacity to heal herself from our exploitation.

The way out is not a way back but the recognition that our tool- and symbol-making skill should be applied to adapting to, not controlling and thereby destroying, the ecosystems in which all life is embedded. For several hundred years, we assumed it possible to enhance civilization and our lives by harnessing the energy of sunlight that fell on the Earth some millions of years ago. We had the dream, and it is close to an end. Technos and Ethos can be brought together in designing a life centered on what is available to us for all time—the energy available from the sun as it is captured by the diverse ecosystems on Earth. That is the true and continuing base for an advanced post-industrial civilization, and it will extend to all our reality as the fossil-fuel age of progress draws to a close.

My own effort has been to create a research institute and a school, where biologists and life scientists, architects, engineers, and craftsmen can come together to plan, build, and live in and evaluate working examples of environments designed to be harmonious with Nature.

The basic sciences, applied sciences, engineering, architecture, and design disciplines are largely creatures and servants of progress culture. Now these disciplines can help to bring into being another kind of environment, another kind of culture. The new culture can combine models of basic nature-related culture with the most imaginative extensions of science, the most creative concepts of design and craft. In cities, suburbs, and the countryside, a new culture can design and live a way of life where the requirements of habitat (shelter, sustenance, sociability) are intimately related to managing the land and its resources, conserving and enhancing the natural ecosystem.

By bringing together people (scientists, engineers, designers, and craftsmen) who share common ideals and complementary skills, the institute will enhance options for ways of life and patterns of land and resource use that:

1. Conserve energy and improve the quality of life through the design of techniques that permit a shift to an economy based on renewable sources of energy.
2. Promote small-scale enterprise, diversity, community, autonomy, and self-reliance.
3. Are humanly satisfying.
4. Respect our dependence on nature.

Natural Design focuses on the design of techniques appropriate to small-scale, stable, self-replenishing systems in which human living and work space, food and energy production, and the natural ecosystem are designed as a single directly connected system.

A Naturally Designed environment will:

1. Use up fewer nonrenewable resources.
2. Rely more on "income" energy from sun, wind, water, and organic sources.
3. Provide its inhabitants with a closer contact with natural cycles, whether in the city or country.
4. Involve inhabitants directly in providing for many of their own needs.
5. Be in harmony with its natural surroundings.
6. Blur the distinction between production and consumption, work, play, and learning.
7. Strive for esthetic, emotional, and spiritual satisfaction.

Further Reading: The Seminal Books of the Seventies

Soft Energy Paths: Towards a Durable Peace
by Amory B. Lovins, 1979

A Pattern Language: Towns, Buildings, Construction
by Christopher Alexander, Sara Ishikawa, Murray Silverstein, 1977

Small is Beautiful: Economics as if People Mattered
by E. F. Schumacher, 1975

The Limits to Growth
by Donella H. Meadows, Dennis L. Meadows, Jørgen Randers, and William W. Behrens III, 1972

The Sixties: Questioning the Dominant World View, Ethos, and Paradigm

The early 1960s continued the material growth model of the 1950s, with continued suburbanization and its infrastructure of freeways and malls subsidized by federal and state governments; a family focus on acquiring more stuff; and a growing middle class. Architects were busy with designing corporate offices, schools, college campuses, hotels, and leisure facilities. The Cold War bubbled with the Cuban Missile Crisis and the Civil Rights Movement showed its face. The assassination of John F. Kennedy shook the nation. Lyndon Johnson used the opportunity to initiate a "War on Poverty" and also stumbled into a major war in Asia that conscripted hundreds of thousands of young men into the military. The War on Poverty gave a highly visible face to the significant percentage of poor people in the United States, particularly African Americans and Latinos. The Civil Rights Movement brought into vivid focus a hundred years of segregation and discrimination against people of color. The Vietnam War drew increasing opposition, particularly among the young. Books such as Rachel Carson's *Silent Spring* exposed the dangers posed to the planet and human health by the massive use of industrial chemicals and a rapidly growing population.

In Berkeley, the Free Speech Movement sprung up after the University of California prohibited student groups from setting up tables in a campus public area to recruit other students to work on civil rights campaigns in the South, while at the same time permitting other groups to recruit students for less politically provocative causes. An increasing number of bright, well-off students began to question the underlying assumptions and operations of the institutions that ran "The Greatest Nation in the World." A "hippie culture" seemed to emerge almost simultaneously, displaying an "alternative life" from that of the great American Dream.

As a young architect, I was always asking why we were doing what we were doing. Why are we designing schools with no windows? "Because there would be no opportunity for bored students to distract themselves by looking out the windows!" Why are we doing a master plan for a major shopping center on a farm site?" Because the client hoped the site would be a new freeway interchange for the adjacent new suburb so he could sell the farm rezoned as a "mall site" for big bucks to the State Highway Department. I wanted my freedom to ask "Why?" and seek my own answers. In 1961, I was appointed to the Berkeley faculty.

The 1960s essays, the "Dorms at Berkeley" monograph, the work with Sandy Hirshen to design and build innovative new communities for California migrant farm workers (an effort funded by Office of Economic Opportunity [OEO], the agency that managed the War on Poverty), and a major grant from the National Institute of Mental Health in 1968 to conduct studies of "New Institutional Forms"—all grew from my "Why?" questions.

The 1960s essays cover a variety of topics, including architectural education: "The design sequences in our schools have become little more than a 10-semester course in architectural cartooning." A second essay, "The University Environment," points out that, everywhere, campuses are being designed and built that "conform to outdated ideas about people, learning, and institutions ... Today's new educational buildings are usually too permanent, heavy, and fixed. They look as though they were designed to last forever. Educational monuments, like the pyramids, reflect the arrogance and faith of their builders in an unchanging world." Several pieces published by the American Institute of Architects in the *AIA Journal* offer that if architecture is to truly consider itself both art and science, it needs to test design ideas and ideologies through deep and impartial evaluation of completed buildings, a process that would eventually become known as "post-occupancy evaluation." Fifty years later, we're still waiting.

"Building a People's Park," Berkeley, CA, 1969

"Judging from my patients," said a psychiatrist friend of mine as we looked back at Berkeley from his sailboat on the bay, "I'd say that 100,000 people mentally shoot down that damned helicopter every day." It was a beautiful day on the water, but full of gallows humor. Not many words were exchanged between the six people on the boat but every now and then someone would take a hard look at the distant shore. You could pick out the white slim shaft of the campanile on the campus, the buildings on the hill at the radiation laboratory. A wisp of smoke curled from somewhere in the industrial area. "Well, I guess Berkeley's burning," said one of the crew, an IBM salesman. "Yeah, here comes the napalm," I said, pointing to a low-flying plane, probably a "weekend warrior" from nearby Alameda Naval Air Station.

I felt weary and heavy that long day on the water. Was my life, as I had known it, going to end? The polarization would continue. Was I going to have to look at everyone, as I now did on the boat, and ask whether they were friend or enemy? Were those smiling young executives in the boat now off our portside going to smile while my life and values would slowly be crushed under the plastic boots of Reaganism? Outside Berkeley, and here on the smiling Saturday waters of San Francisco Bay, life went on as usual. But anguished liberals in Berkeley were smarting under the first tentative thrusts of fascism. The police state had moved out of the ghetto and into a university town. Civil rights had been repeatedly violated and innocent people had been seriously injured and even killed. Normal life in the city had come to a standstill. But few liberals outside Berkeley seemed to care or understand. Yes, my friends in Palo Alto would contribute to the bail fund. Yes, conditions at the prison farm where they hauled off 800 young people were shocking. There would have to be an investigation by the authorities who run the place. But after all, squatting on university property was going a bit too far. And all that fuss about a park! It was going too far. It was natural that if the students and hippies rocked the boat too much, the reactionaries would seize the opportunity to embarrass the liberal establishment. It was better to work through channels. I finally understood why blacks reserved their maximum contempt for liberals.

The capacity for we liberals to delude ourselves about our institutions and democracy seemed limitless. For years we had tolerated a police state in the ghetto. We had done everything through legal and constitutional channels to end racism and repression. But even the Kerner Report had said that conditions were only getting worse. We had stood back and watched in horror as Malcolm X, John F. Kennedy, Martin Luther King, and Robert Kennedy had been eliminated. We had joked Ronnie Reagan

all the way into the state house in Sacramento. We hadn't believed Tricky Dick could make it. We had talked, convened, resolved, sought redress.

It wasn't working. It hadn't worked. And now the nightmare was coming true. The cancer we had tolerated too long in the ghetto had moved into a peaceful university town. And all it had taken was a small plot of land, what the kids had called a People's Park, to bring on the horror.

I had first heard about the park some time during April, from a student who was helping build it. Then, on the Monday following the first weekend of park building, I visited the site. I remember being amazed to see what for nine months had been a dusty rutted parking lot now transformed, with sod and flowers, into a pleasant place to be. At the impromptu bulletin board tacked onto a power pole on the site I ran into Bill Miller, whom I knew only by sight. Bill is in his thirties, powerfully built, balding with scraggly shoulder-length blond hair, clear blue eyes, and missing some of his front teeth. I knew Bill had been active in the community for some years. He had run a free bus service from San Francisco to Berkeley until his old school bus ran into trouble from the highway patrol. He now owned a store on the street and had run unsuccessfully for city council in the previous spring elections. He was dressed in a yellow-fringed shirt and rawhide leather vest and bell-bottoms. He and several others were talking about raising money from merchants to buy some more sod to lay the following week. I reached for my wallet and handed him ten dollars. He asked for my name to enter it and the amount of the donation in a lined school notebook he was carrying. Hearing my name, he mentioned he had heard of me through a mutual friend. We talked a bit about their plans for the park and he mentioned that there would be a meeting at his house that evening to discuss the continuing development of the park.

When I arrived at the address Bill had given me, neither the house nor the meeting met my expectations. Although I considered myself knowledgeable about the Telegraph Avenue scene and fairly hip, I hadn't known anyone who was actively involved in it. I knew that Bill operated a sort of commune and expected to enter a decrepit, "groovy" pad with the psychedelic posters, furnishings, and sleeping bags strewn about. Instead, the house was a comfortable, well-maintained one along Fraternity Row, conventionally furnished and much neater than most fraternity houses I had been in. There were coffee and donuts on the dining room table. In the front room, about 40 people were gathered, mostly long-haired. Mike Delacour, whom I had met with Bill in the park, was standing with one foot on a chair in the corner leading the discussion. They were discussing how to keep cars from parking on the portion of the site they were working on. After several minutes it was decided that one person each morning would take the responsibility to get to the park at 6:00 a.m. and keep the cars out.

The discussion turned to buying and storing additional tools for the following weeks' work, and collecting money. A strikingly vibrant blond, Wendy Schlessinger, gave an articulate account of their door-to-door fund-raising operation among merchants. Others discussed leafleting the local neighborhood to involve more residents in building the park. The issue of an overall plan for the park was raised by Max Scherr, the middle-aged owner and publisher of the *Berkeley Barb*, an underground newspaper, which reportedly makes Scherr a profit of some $5000 a week. Scherr, round-faced, steel-rim glasses perched on his nose, full beard and workman's cap, believed there should be an overall plan to insure some sort of esthetic standard. I found this strange coming from Scherr, whose anarchic paper is probably the ugliest tabloid in the underground press. Scherr's concern was dismissed by the group, which believed that a plan was contrary to the spirit and purpose of a park, where each person could be creative and get others to work on an idea if he could convince them of its value.

I found myself pleasantly surprised and fascinated by the meeting. I hadn't looked forward to going to another boring meeting but had gone out of curiosity. As a professor I was used to going to endless unproductive meetings where carefully hedged words tended to be used to protect people's territories and mask particular positions. The faculty in my experience was not fond of the phrases "I feel" or "I need." They preferred more comfortable abstractions such as "It is necessary." Faculty committees often fumbled through an agenda on a perfunctory basis, the conversation too often directed at the chairman and not at other members. Here, however, was a group of people who appeared to share a common purpose, had real respect for each other but were not afraid to disagree. Their speech was articulate and direct. The chairman simply "orchestrated" the meeting and kept it on focus. Later I was to find out that anyone at such a meeting could assume the role of chairman or leader. Those who were good at it assumed the role more often than others, although there was no particular power or political position attached to being "the chairman." As the meeting continued, the question came up, what about the university? I got up and said, "I'm Sim Van der Ryn, and I have some connections with the chancellor's office." That was the wrong thing to say, and there was some hissing even then. Then I said that I would be happy to try and do what I could. They didn't seem very interested.

On May 7, I finally got hold of the vice-chancellor of student affairs and told him about the People's Park. Very soon thereafter, the chancellor, Roger Heyns, asked me to come by his office and discuss the matter. But apparently our discussion had little effect, because the next day Heyns sent a memorandum to some of the park people, warning them of the consequences if they continued their work.

On Friday I went over to the park. Mike Delacour was there. The conditions of the memorandum were clearly unacceptable to them. And yet, Delacour and the others started to understand that at least I was really with them, that I was trying to buy time for them. I had thought that, as chairman of the Chancellor's Advisory Committee on Housing and Environment, I could have some effect. Now I had been proven wrong. The kids understood.

On Wednesday evening around 11:00, the night before the fence was erected, I went over to the park with Jon Read, a landscape architect and contractor who had been a driving force in building the park, both in organizing work and providing much-needed advice on all kinds of technical matters. The park was quiet. About 100 people were seated in the "amphitheatre," a hollowed-out oval that had started out as a fishpond but then became an amphitheatre after several on-site debates about the hazards of children falling in ponds and the difficulty of keeping the water fresh. The people, mostly young, were sitting quietly with hands linked. A handsome young black student with a lilting voice, Gene, was good-naturedly getting the group "synched in"—that is, getting people to really feel each other's psychic and physical presence. He would squeeze the hand of the person next to him and then wait for the impulse to be telegraphed around the circle to come back to him in his other hand. With so many people, it took a long time for the message to get back to Gene; sometimes it didn't get back at all, and Gene gently chided the group, "Come on now, let's get with it—let's really move it around." The group was having a good time. There was a sense of joy and community that I had never seen on campus. It reminded me of pleasurable times with good friends around a campfire in the Sierra. Close by, a smaller group was standing around a fire. It's strange, I thought, that after all our modern "improvements," we haven't managed to improve on the atavistic urge to share

a campfire, to share memories and feelings staring into the flames. Of course there was an ordinance against campfires in city parks. Looking around the park, I realized how its forms were more natural, more functional, and comfortable than the usual fixtures of the public park: the seesaws were built of weathered rounded lumber, not cold steel pipe. The benches were slabs of worn and hollowed redwood, not hard cement. The amphitheatre was beautifully suited to its purpose: an irregular oval growing into the ground with several tiers of seats.

What did that last night in the park have to do with the university? Why was I there? Why was I having a good time with kids half my age?

The next day was Bloody Thursday.

The storm that raged through Berkeley's streets for the next weeks alarmed, surprised, and frightened liberals like myself, most of whom had been sitting comfortably in modern homes on the hills since the Free Speech Movement of 1964. Of course, there had been people like Fred Cody, the Telegraph Avenue bookseller, who for years had been working to meet the youth problems of the South Campus area. But attempts at trying to generate creative responses from the city and other sources had failed. Now there was a crisis, and we liberals found ourselves hopelessly impotent.

The liberal demise had been gradual. No sooner had we congratulated ourselves on fully integrating the schools several years before than we began to be alarmed about "falling academic standards." No sooner had we begun to pride ourselves on our non-authoritarian and "progressive" techniques for dealing with our children than we began to worry about the children's lack of motivation toward college and professional careers. No sooner had we boasted about our level of tolerance for novelty and non-conformity in our community than we became concerned over the hippie transformation of "Constitution Park," a square block of green across from Berkeley City Hall, into what even the Mayor now called "Provo Park," where free food was often dispensed from garbage cans and where marijuana was smoked with impunity. The consequences of liberal responses during the past few years had revealed a dilemma.

Most of us had been content to live in pleasant homes on shady streets running over the hills north and east of the campus. We had left the management of community affairs to others. We had a nice backyard view of the Bay—at least on windy days, when the pall of smog didn't obscure everything. For most people in the city, life was good. We closed our eyes to the shoddy new construction, the elimination of fine old homes, the deterioration of a pleasant environment. But now things were getting out of hand. Phenomenal overrun costs on the Bay Area Rapid Transit District had caused taxes to rise sharply, and the system appeared to have been a gigantic white elephant. The city was developing a marina for private commercial interests while Berkeley only had a tenth of the park area per person of nearby Palo Alto. And today helicopters were dumping tear gas onto the campus, and the painfully pungent smell was already spreading onto the shady streets and into the pleasant homes. The liberal hypocrisy could no longer be ignored.

As the sound of the National Guard trucks rumbling through the streets mixed with the constant drone of the helicopter, and the sight of police dressed in flak jackets and holding shotguns contrasted with views of running, frightened kids, I, for one, began to understand my own liberal lip-service. Many friends said later that the People's Park experience had "radicalized" me. How could I tell them that I had only grown to realize the emptiness of liberal maxims devoid of the hard, gut action needed to see them through to their ends?

"Problems and Puzzles," AIA Journal, January 1966

When Walter Gropius came to the United States in 1937 he wrote, "My intention is not to introduce a cut and dried Modern Style from Europe but rather to introduce a method of approach which allows one to tackle a problem according to its peculiar conditions." This intent has not been realized. Concern for "a method of approach" remains in the realm of the personal rather than public knowledge and is not really part of any modern theory of design. Modern architecture is entering its third generation. Its major concern of the past 50 years has been the technology of building and its resultant form. The modern theory of architecture is a theory of immediate and material form, its emphasis a response to the great nineteenth-century advances in the production and technology of material wealth. But advances in the material advances of architecture have been at the expense of understanding the process of design and extension of design theory.

Despite the intellect and energies of Gropius and other modern-movement leaders, the way in which architects approach problems is often much the same as it was before the advent of the modern movement. Yes the nature of design problems has changed drastically. There is in this third generation of modern architecture both the need and the opportunity to make profound changes in theory and practice. The new architecture established principles and gave a new conception against which our efforts are still measured. But the configuration of change in society has been so great, while the old landmarks guide us along a few well-traveled and familiar paths toward solutions. In design or any other human activity in which ethics and values play a crucial part, a time-lag is found between the realities of a dynamic society and the perceptions, principles, and practices of a particular discipline. The new architecture was a landmark because it settled the score with what was already accomplished fact: the great age of the machine and its triumphs of production—a triumph shared by reasoned orderly science wedded to an economy bent on the production of material wealth. In responding to the potentials of the already well-established technology, the pioneers of the modern movement realized that before they could meet the challenge of the future, they had to catch up with the past. Even as they formulated concepts and translated them into buildings, profound changes in the images that guide men's actions were occurring. Nineteenth-century science, a world of material science and total explanation, perhaps epitomized by Kelvin's remark that no phenomenon could be understood unless it could be represented by an actual mechanical model, was being superseded by the new conceptions of Einstein, Planck, and others. The new scientific conception viewed order as the expression of probability, time, and space as not absolutes, and events not always capable of translation into mechanical terms. Although Gropius and his colleagues were familiar with then emerging views of life and society which have greatly affected our lives, they were busy rescuing design from a static, anachronistic state. This strategy demanded a practical attitude oriented towards the immediate technical and spatial problems of building. The creation of a visibly new order of form was crucial. At the Bauhaus, Gropius intended that process, product, and use constitute an inseparable entity in modern design. But the momentum for change in method as well as matter was dispersed and diluted in the trauma of war and its aftermath. A world busy rebuilding, expanding, and shaping its environments adopted the products of modern architecture, but not its budding methods. The communication of an approach toward design has been distorted in the communication of styles. Method remains a personally derived resource rather than a known quality available to the designer. The failure of modern theory to include a theory of method has led to inaction and failure on the problem the makers of the modern movement saw as their greatest challenge: the design of humane urban environments.

The failure of physical designers to deal effectively with large-scale design issues, or to create solutions acceptable to society, is a failure of method and strategy and not of good intentions or interest. We have been busy studying solutions but seldom problems. The special skill the designer must have is to discover problems and their conceptual solutions. The designer is first and last a problem-solver in which physical form is the medium of solution. The development of problem-solving skills in theory and practice can be approached with the same kind of care that we have lavished on questions of immediate form. We have thought too long of architecture as a fixed and static product about which we can learn only through the photograph, the plan, without considering the form of the problem itself, the needs which required solution, the process of discovery, creation, and use.

A unified theory of design must deal with form and three levels or stages of action. At the first, or preform stage of design, we are concerned with discovering the nature of the design problem. The second phase of design deals with the technical means of implementing form. The third phase is concerned with evaluating solutions. Design is a continuum of processes, a chain of development, realization and evaluation, directed toward the purposeful creation of physical form. The present state of design theory, by atomizing the design process and concentrating only on physical realization, does not lead to an extension of design knowledge. There is a major difference between our current loosely organized design profession operating with a minimum of theory and relying on ad hoc methods, and a design institution with an internal structure focused on systemically extending knowledge through systemic research.

Science is most successful in the systemic extension of knowledge. Design cannot imitate science nor ignore it. The two are complementary activities. Contrary to popular misconception, the scientific method does not limit the innovation of ideas or the creative solution of problems. It is simply a method to test the usefulness of creative hypotheses. Any physical form is the synthesis of numerous hypotheses which predict events in the real world. Any physical form is a model which seeks to predict events in the real world, and thus a symbolic as well as a physical entity.

The extent to which a particular physical innovation or design is successful is measured by the extent to which the hypotheses contained in its conception successfully predicts the reality of its use. Any physical form is a container for numerous

implicit hypotheses about human behavior: assumptions about how the building will work for a given activity or event. During the first phase of design, collaboration between architects, clients, designated users, and social scientists is essential in agreeing on the building program which must include clear statements of specific hypotheses regarding desired performance outcomes in human terms.

If we set about to systemically develop design hypotheses, build them into solutions and then test them in the light of reality, we begin to construct a unified theory of design which permits us to identify and face design problems in our society in a purposeful and meaningful way. The centrality of design to society is directly proportional to the design profession's record of proven success, its potential to solve with proven predictability particular kinds of design problems and issues. Since there is little consensus about the specific objectives of design stated in a way that results can be meaningfully measured, the effects of design are seldom assessed, and the human and monetary costs of individual and collective failure are seldom measured. A design system must include the means to assess the effects of our work. If we were able to measure the costs of design failure as we do the costs of failure in the space program, the true importance of environmental design to society would become apparent. What are the physical and social costs of failures in environmental design: the costs to our mental and physical health, discomforts heaped on us by ill-design?

If we have no predictable theory of design other than the technology of building, then technology will continue to serve as an attractive end to the exclusion of broader design questions. If the values which we seek to satisfy remain vague and incapable of clear definition, then we cannot act on them purposefully, and we will continue to focus on technology as an end in itself. In proposing the concept of a unified theory of design, we assume that physical form and the structure and nature of activities for which we designed, comprise a single inseparable entity. Ever increasing technological skills must proceed hand in hand with the corresponding development of design science that can predict human behavior in designed environments through a process of formulating hypotheses, embodying them in physical solutions, obtaining objective information on the performance of solutions, and evaluating and updating the hypotheses. A unified theory of design would expect to see a wider scope of specialization in the design professions and their integration into a collaborative design process. The model of the designer postulated by the modern movement was that of the master builder who combines the qualities of designer, builder, and businessman. The mix between design, technique, and research would vary with each professional competent in at least one of the three stages of design.

Perhaps most symptomatic of the absence of an institution of design is the condition of its foundation—the educational system. Unlike every other professional activity, the schools of architecture and design have failed since the Bauhaus to be centers for the production, extension, and communication of design knowledge. The failure to extend knowledge, channel information, and create significant theory is a reflection on the state of development in design programs. The challenge for change and the development of a unified theory rests with the profession as a whole and particularly with its educational system.

Further Reading: The Seminal Books of the Sixties

Mechanization Takes Command: A Contribution to Anonymous History
by Siegfried Giedion, 1969

The Whole Earth Catalog, 1968 and 1969

The Population Bomb
by Paul R. Ehrlich, 1968

Silent Spring
by Rachel Carson, 1962

Index

agribusiness 115, 119
air conditioning 23–4, 58, 86
Alameda Naval Air Station 139
Alexander, C. 61–2, 133
aliveness 45–6
Ambrose, S. 58
American Civil War 85
American Institute of Architects (AIA) 24, 138
Arcologies 118
Arizona 36, 47
Arks 9, 45, 88, 115
assembly lines 40
assumptions 18, 23
Athena Award Reception Speech 14–15

Bateson Building Dedication 105–6
Bateson, G. 10, 105–6
Bauhaus 69, 149, 152
Beaux Arts 67
beginner's mind 40, 46
Behrens, W. W. III 133
Benyus, J. 19, 37, 63
Berry, T. 18, 63
Berry, W. 38, 51, 99
bioclimatics 23
biodiversity 20, 41, 47
biomes 51
biomorphism 51
bionauts 36
biophilia 6, 19
biosphere 45, 50
Biosphere II 36, 47, 60
biotecture 70
Brand, S. 8, 10, 94, 109
Britain *see* United Kingdom
Broadacre City 113
Brown, G. 67
Brown, J. 104, 106, 109
Buddhism 94
budgets 51, 87, 90, 106
bureaucracy 78, 104, 113, 122, 126, 130

California 5, 18, 24, 33–4, 45; eighties 69, 79, 86–91, 94–5; seventies 103–5, 109, 119, 122, 130–1; sixties 137

Calthorpe, P. 8, 14, 28, 67
Campus Sustainability Committee 24
capitalism 11, 36, 40, 47
carbon footprint 6
carbon sinks 58
Carson, R. 137, 154
Carter, J. 67, 108
Cascadia Green Building Council 6–12
cells 75, 78
census data 89
Center for Ecoliteracy 33
Centers of Life 61–2
certification 19
charrettes 54
China 82, 115, 127
Chua, A. 9
cities 8, 10, 15, 22, 44; eighties 70, 78–9, 85; nineties 44, 47–60; seventies 127
climate dynamics 10–11
climate-responsive design 106
code barriers 5
Cody, F. 146
co-evolution 45–6
Cold War 137
Coming Age of Natural Design 126–32
commodities 19, 37, 50, 59
Commoner, B. 113
conscious community 123
conservation 44, 62, 71, 74, 88, 108–9, 112, 132
corporations 5, 11, 15, 18, 51; eighties 89–90, 94; nineties 59; seventies 115, 130; sixties 137
Cowan, S. 33
Cuban Missile Crisis 137
cubicle farms 54
cultural memes 18

Daly, G. 36
Darwinism 45, 90
debt 8
de-carbonization 38, 58
Dederich, C. 89
defoliants 95
Delacour, M. 142–3
dematerialization 37–8, 51, 58–9

INDEX

Democrats 90
denial 9, 15, 25
Descartes, R. 86
design ecotones 41–4
Diamond, J. 9, 25, 28
Dogon people 45

Earth Day 103
EcoDesign 19
ecofundamentalism 10
ecoliteracy 24–5, 33, 37
ecologic 25
ecological accounting 19
Ecological Cities Conference 47–60
ecological design 5, 19–20, 37–8, 50, 54–5, 62, 113–15, 123
Ecological Design Institute 33
ecological footprint 6, 38, 54–5, 58
ecology 36–7, 47, 50–4, 70–1, 74; eighties 95, 98; seventies 103–4, 112–13, 122–3
ecomorphism 51
economics 18, 36–7, 40, 46–7, 50–1; eighties 75, 79, 82, 98; nineties 59; seventies 115, 126, 130
economy 47, 55, 59, 79, 112; eighties 82; seventies 122, 127, 132; sixties 148
ecostructure 36, 50
ecosystems 46, 75, 78, 83, 87; services 36, 47; seventies 122, 131–2
ecotecture 70
ecotones 41–4, 47, 61
Ecotopia Now 108–23
Ehrlich, P. 113, 154
Eighties 65–8, 90
Elgin, D. 63
emergence 46
energetics 61
energy 7–10, 14, 19, 23–4, 36–8; eighties 67, 69–71, 74–5, 78–9, 82, 85, 87–8, 95; nineties 44, 50–1, 55, 58–9, 61; seventies 104–6, 108–9, 112–15, 118, 122, 126–7, 131–2
Energy Pavilion 103
entropy 44, 61, 70–1, 75, 82, 115
Environmental Design Research Association 18–20
environmentalism 67, 90, 103, 127, 152
epistemology 40, 45
equity 36–7, 47, 50
esthetics 36, 45, 47, 79, 82–3; seventies 106, 113, 115, 122–3, 132; sixties 142
ethics 36, 45, 47, 103, 148
Europe 94, 148
eutrophication 79, 115
evolution 15, 18, 22, 36, 45–6; eighties 70, 74–5, 95; nineties 51, 59–61
experimentation 5, 9–10, 22–3, 103, 118

Farallones Institute 78, 104, 115
Farallones Integral Urban House 10, 78, 88, 104, 114–15, 118
Farallones Rural Center 86, 88, 104, 119
Fathy, H. 130
Fedrizzi, R. 25
Fifties 137
Findhorn 94
flood plains 47
flow 37–8, 45, 47, 50, 54–9; eighties 74–5, 78, 82–3, 98; nineties 62; seventies 106, 112, 115

food chains 71, 74
Ford, H. 40
fossil fuels 6, 10, 14, 23, 71; eighties 82, 85, 87–8; seventies 103, 105, 108, 113, 115, 119, 131
fractal geometry 19
Frenay, R. 19
Friend, R. 91
Friends of the Earth 108
Fuller, B. 9, 37–8, 59, 109
future generations 7, 11, 15, 18, 23; eighties 69, 82, 87–8; nineties 36, 44; seventies 103
Futurism 126

Gaia theory 45
garden cities 112
Gebser, J. 59, 99
genetic engineering 47–50, 55
Giedion, S. 40, 85, 154
global positioning systems (GPS) 58–9
global warming 58
globalization 37, 51
Goerner, S. J. 63
Gottfried, D. 25
government 5, 15, 55, 79, 89; eighties 95, 98; seventies 105, 127; sixties 137
Great Turning 7
Green Gulch Farm 91–2
green roofs 24, 33
Greening Campuses, Greening Education 22–6
Gropius, W. 130, 148–9
Gross Domestic Product (GDP) 37, 50, 62
Gross National Product (GNP) 75
Gross World Product 36, 47
Guitar House 33

Hardin, G. 55
Hawken, A. 91, 94
Hawken, P. 11, 18, 36, 47, 63, 91, 94
Hayes, D. 67, 103
Healthy Building 40–6
heating, ventilation, and air conditioning (HVAC) 58
hegemony 59
Heschel, A. 20
Heyns, R. 143
Hirshen, S. 137
homeostasis 71, 74
homeplace 87–8, 122
Howard, E. 112
human capital 36, 47, 55
Hyams, E. 70–1

Ikat 91
Industrial Revolution 41, 85
innovation 5, 33, 51, 94, 104, 115, 122, 137
integral design 69–83, 104, 112, 118
Integral Urban House (IUH) 10, 78, 88, 104
integrated life cycle costing 38, 58
interdisciplinarity 11
International Living Building Challenge 6
Internet 19, 103
Ishikawa, S. 133

INDEX

Jeavons, J. 119
Johnson, L. B. 137

Kennedy, J.F. 127, 137, 139
Kerner Report 139
Keynesianism 75
Korten, D.C. 63

Leadership in Energy and Environmental Design (LEED) 6, 10–11, 23–5; nineties 33
Le Corbusier 130
liberalism 90, 127, 139, 146
Life Expression Chiropractic Center 33
linear systems 71, 79, 113–15
Little America 89–98
Living Building Challenge 19
living systems design 45, 50, 115
Local Exchange Trading Schemes (LETS) 50
Lovins, A. 108–9, 133
Ludwig, A. 5

McCloskey, P. 103
McIssac, P. 91
McIssac, T. 91
McLennan, J. 6
McLuhan, M. 74
Macy, J. 11, 28
Mann, C. 9
Marin Solar Village Corporation 67
Meadows, D. H. 133
Meadows, D. L. 133
media 18, 89, 103
metabolism 38, 54–5, 58–9, 78
metadisciplinarity 11, 18–19
Mies van der Rohe, L. 130
military 95, 108, 137
Miller, B. 142
mining 25, 87
Mitchell, C. 89
Mitchell, D. 89
Modern Movement 22, 130, 148, 152
monocultures 70–1, 74–5, 82, 119
Moral Majority 90
Myung Jim Handmade Fabrics 91

National Book Award 91
National Institute of Mental Health 137
Native American people 95
natural capital 38, 55, 58, 60
natural design 41, 44, 50–1, 70, 126–32
negentropy 70
Nelson, G. 103
Netherlands 54
New Alchemy Ark 88, 115
New Alchemy Institute 45
New Ruralism 10
New Urbanism 10, 14–15
Next Urban Transformation 85–8
Nineties 32–4
Nixon, R. 90, 103, 142
No Child Left Inside 34

Norway 127

Oasis Design 5
Occidental Arts and Ecology Center 104
Office of Appropriate Technology 104, 109
Office of Economic Opportunity (OEO) 137
Oldenburg, C. 126
O'Neill, G. 108
organic design 44–5, 70, 130
organic food 34, 86, 127
organisms 75, 78
Orr, D. 18
outcomes 51
outlaw communities 94
outsourcing 5

Pasteur, L. 85
Pattern Language 61
Peace Corps 67
people 50–4
People's Park 103, 139–46
Perennial Philosophy 18
Pilloton, E. 28
Pillsbury, C.A. 40
place 50–4
Platinum Plus 24
politics 6, 18, 59, 90, 94, 113, 130
pollution 6, 9, 14, 59, 79, 86, 90
population 8, 14, 40, 71, 75; eighties 89; seventies 103, 113; sixties 137
post-occupancy evaluation 33, 138
Problems and Puzzles 148–52
profit 5, 8, 14, 79, 142
progress 115–22, 126–7, 130–1
prototypes 115–22
psychology 54, 118, 127
Pulitzer Prize 89
pulse 38, 50–60, 82, 115
pyramid schemes 95

Quality of Life index 37, 50

radicalism 6, 33
Randers, J. 133
Read, J. 143
Reagan, R. 67, 103, 105, 139
Redefining Progress 37, 50
regeneration 8–10, 25, 44, 62
regulation 5, 55
Republicans 90
resilience 8–10, 15
restoration 8–10, 25
Robertson, C. 91
Robertson, J. 91
Rocky Mountain Institute 24
Rodale, B. 62
Romanticism 50
Roshi, S. 40
Royal Institute of British Architects (RIBA) 68
Rudofsky, B. 130
Ruskin, J. 37, 50

INDEX

Russia 89, 95

San Domenico School 33–4
San Francisco Zen Center 94
scale integration 18, 20, 37, 47, 75
Scherr, M. 142
Schlessinger, W. 142
Schumacher, E. F. 7, 133
Schumacher, P. 68
Scotland 94
September 11 2001 5
Seventies 94, 101, 103–4
Sightline.org 5
Silent Majority 90
Silverstein, M. 133
Sixties 90, 94–5, 127, 135, 137–8
skyscrapers 15
Solar Aquacell System 119, 122
Solar Energy Association of Oregon 36–8
Solar Energy Research Institute (SERI) 67
Solar Living Center 24, 33
Soleri, P. 118
Space Colony 108–9
stakeholders 19, 54
Straus, R. 9
Sullivan, L. 37, 50
surpassability 15
Surplus Property Act 67
survivalism 10
sustainability 5–6, 10, 12, 20, 22; definitions 8, 14–15; eighties 67, 85, 87–8; nineties 33, 36–8, 44, 47, 50, 58, 61–2; role 24–5; seventies 112, 122
Switzerland 50
Synanon 89

technology 8, 11, 15, 22, 25; eighties 67–8, 71, 85, 87–8, 94–5; nineties 36–8, 40–1, 47, 58, 60; seventies 104, 108–9, 112–13, 118–19, 122, 126–7; sixties 148, 152
templates 40
Tennessee Valley Authority (TVA) 75

Thompson, W. I. 15, 99
thought experiments 9
Todd, J. 45
Todd, N. 45
Tolle, E. 11, 15
tragedy of the commons 55
Transformation 6–12
triple bottom line 22
Two-thousands 4–6

unemployment 6
United Kingdom (UK) 68, 112
United States Green Building Council (USGBC) 6, 23, 25, 33
United States Public Building Service 25
United States (US) 5–6, 8, 37, 40, 55; eighties 67–8, 82–3, 85, 89–98; seventies 103–4, 115, 119, 127, 131; sixties 137, 148
urban revitalization 112–13
Urban Transformation 85–8
urbanism 14–15
utopianism 108–23

Valpey, G. 33
Vietnam 95, 127, 137

Wackernagel, M. 58
Wall Street 8–9
wars 90, 95, 106, 127, 137, 149
watercolor sketching 67
Watt, J. 90
wetlands 37, 41, 50, 54, 67, 86
Whole Earth Catalog 94, 109, 127, 154
Whole Systems 9, 86, 104
wholeness 45–6
wilderness 41
World War II 23
Wright, F.L. 20, 112–13, 130

Zen 40, 94
zoning 44

T - #0072 - 260922 - C176 - 276/216/10 - PB - 9780415839679 - Gloss Lamination